Robert Stuart MacArthur

The celestial Lamp

And other Sermons

Robert Stuart MacArthur

The celestial Lamp
And other Sermons

ISBN/EAN: 9783337116880

Printed in Europe, USA, Canada, Australia, Japan

Cover: Foto ©ninafisch / pixelio.de

More available books at **www.hansebooks.com**

THE CELESTIAL LAMP

AND

OTHER SERMONS

BY
ROBERT STUART MACARTHUR

As thieves be loath to assault a house where they know there be good armor and artillery, so wherever the books of the Holy Scripture be well occupied and exercised, there neither the devil nor any of his angels dare come near.
—*Cawdray*

PHILADELPHIA
AMERICAN BAPTIST PUBLICATION SOCIETY
1420 Chestnut Street

Copyright 1899 by the
AMERICAN BAPTIST PUBLICATION SOCIETY

From the Society's own Press

PREFACE

WITH the exception of the anniversary sermons, those contained in this volume were preached on consecutive Sundays in the Calvary Baptist Church, New York, in the regular work of the author's pastorate. It will be observed that several sermons give special prominence to various characteristics of the word of God.

It is the author's hope and prayer that the pathway of all readers may be illumined by "The Celestial Lamp" until they walk in "The Perfected Light," and finally attain "The Realized Ideal."

ROBERT STUART MACARTHUR.

CALVARY STUDY, NEW YORK, July, 1899.

CONTENTS

SERMON	PAGE
I. The Celestial Lamp	9
II. The Fruitful Word	29
III. The Resistless Weapon	47
IV. The Inspired "Withouts"	63
V. The Defensible Hope	81
VI. The Christian Graces	97
VII. The Desirable Growth	113
VIII. The Ephesian Prayer	131
IX. The Eternal Paradox	147
X. The Grateful Exhortation	165
XI. The Certain Evidence	183
XII. The Tested Discipleship	201
XIII. The Inestimable Possession	219
XIV. The Rescued Disciple	237
XV. The Philippian Prayer	255
XVI. The Triumphant Worshipers	273

SERMON	PAGE
XVII. THE JUBILEE YEAR	291
XVIII. THE DIVINE FORGIVENESS	313
XIX. THE PERFECTED LIGHT	329
XX. THE REALIZED IDEAL	347

I

THE CELESTIAL LAMP

"Thy word is a lamp unto my feet, and a light unto my path." Ps. 119 : 105.

I

THIS great psalm is an alphabetical psalm; and it is the longest and most perfect of its kind in the psalter. Its peculiarity is that in the original Hebrew the first eight verses begin with the first letter of the alphabet; the next eight verses with the second letter, and so on through the twenty-two letters of that alphabet. In the third chapter of the Lamentations of Jeremiah we have a somewhat similar arrangement. But there the stanzas consist of only three verses, while here each stanza consists of eight verses, and each verse of two members. Other instances of this acrostic arrangement are found in the psalter.

The subject of this psalm is the law of God considered as the rule of life. The excellency of this law is set forth with great fullness, and the benefit of its observance is emphasized with equal earnestness and variety of language. It is remarkable that one subject can be presented in so many lights, and from so many points of view as is here done in the course of these one hundred and seventy-six verses.

It was long ago pointed out that there is only one verse, the one hundred and twenty-second, which does not contain some reference to, or description of, the law of God. These references are made under some one of ten names, corresponding, it is supposed, to the Ten Words or commands which make up the Decalogue. The psalm is really an elaboration of the closing part of the nineteenth Psalm which, it will be remembered, is a statement of the characteristics, the excellences, and the blessed effects of the law of the Lord. The text reminds us that what a torch is to a man in a dark night, the word of God is to a man in life's night and on life's journey. It prevents him from stumbling over obstacles which are lying in his path; it enables him to see and so to avoid precipices over which he might fall to certain destruction. The language is as beautiful rhetorically as it is instructive spiritually. The word of God is heaven's benediction to humanity. This truth will appear the more clearly as we study the influence of the Bible in several departments of life's activity.

I. THE BIBLE AND LITERATURE. The influence of the Bible on literature is worthy of our most careful consideration. This is a day of the making and reading of many books. Every age produces its supply. Solomon said, about three thousand years ago, "Of making many books there is no end"; were he living now he would write that sentence in large capitals. But the majority of books die with the age which gives them birth. Many of them ought to die; they are bad, and that continually. It is impossible to read all the books published by the prolific press of the day; and it is as undesirable as it is impossible. As well might you submit to having every man you meet on Broadway to-morrow morning take you by the button-hole, as have every book published arrest your attention. There are, however, certain classics that every well-informed man should read. There are works of history, science, art, and fiction which all intelligent men must read. The books that are like "the tree of life which bare twelve manner of fruits, and yielded her fruit every month; and the leaves of the tree were for the healing of the nations," will survive.

There is in literature a law of "the survival of the fittest." The worst portions of Byron and Shelley practically will be unread as the years multiply; only their nobler parts will endure. A good book is a wonderful product of brain and heart. Milton uttered a great truth when he said, "Books are not absolutely dead things, but do contain a progeny of life in them to be as active as that soul was whose progeny they are; nay, they do preserve as in a vial the purest efficacy and extraction of that living intellect that bred them. A good book is the precious life-blood of a master-spirit, embalmed and treasured up on purpose to a life beyond life." These true and strong words are especially applicable to the Bible, which by pre-eminence is called "The Book." Every student of life and literature, whatever his religious opinions may be, ought to be deeply interested in the Bible. It is a book of greater antiquity than any other; it is more widely read than any other; and it exercises a more potent influence on thought and life than any other book. It commands the love and evokes the hostility of more people than any other volume in the world. It comes to us with the loftiest pretensions, and it demands for its message our absolute acceptance. It is the only unexhausted and inexhaustible book in the world. As the intelligence of its readers enlarges, so does its significance enlarge and its beauty increase. In itself and in its history it is the mightiest force in literature.

It consists of two volumes, one of thirty-nine and the other of twenty-seven books. It took sixteen hundred years to make it. It has about forty human authors; and it was written in somewhat different countries, as well as in widely different centuries. It discusses many subjects, but it preserves perfect unity throughout. Its unity has been appropriately and eloquently illustrated by the keynote in a grand oratorio. That keynote is now heard thundering in the bass, now trembling in the soprano, and now for a moment it is lost to hearing; but it is ever appearing until it reasserts itself in a magnificent outburst of harmony. In like manner the predominating thought of the Bible is seen in history, in prophecy, in petition, and in doxology. It is an internal rather than an external unity. It is the unity of some glorious castle or some ancient cathedral. Although cathedral and castle externally may represent different centuries, different architects, and various styles of architecture, yet the interior often shows the dominance of one great thought, and all parts of the edifice contribute to one definite purpose.

The authors of the Bible differed widely from one another. Some were princes, some peasants; some were warriors, some lovers of peace; some lived in palaces, and some in tents. But all were actuated by one spirit; all worked according to one great plan of the one divine Author. There may be in the Bible an absence of system; but there is the presence of method. Systems are human; methods are divine. You find methods in rocks and fields; you find systems in museums and herbariums. It might have been enough for the principles of revelation if God had made the book simply instructive; but he is pleased also to make it attractive. Like God's other volume, the book of nature, it has its lofty mountains, its shady dells, its suns and stars, its smiling fields, and its singing groves.

If we think of the history contained in the Bible we shall be able the better to judge of its value to literature. It is the earliest record of the oldest events; it reaches to the morning of creation. It leads us through all the eras of creation until man appears as the crowning glory of God's creative work. It permits us to hear the morning stars singing together; it gives us the first notes of praise uttered by the joyous sons of God. Not Herodotus, but Moses, is the true "Father of History." The book is largely composed of history and biography, and no studies are more important than these. Carlyle said that the only true history is biography; and in this respect the Bible surpasses all other books. It avoids the dangers and it illustrates the excellences of this most difficult kind of writing.

Let us think, also, of its poetry, that we may the better appreciate its relations to literature. What is poetry? That is a difficult question. In a little volume, to which I am indebted for some of these allusions and illustrations, entitled, "The Claims of the Bible," by Mr. William Walters, there are some answers to this question. Aristotle says, "Poetry is imitation"; the quaint Thomas Fuller says, "Poetry is music in words"; and Dr. Johnson defines poetry to be, "The art of pleasing." Shakespeare and Cowper have endeavored to define poetry, but probably neither they nor any others can give a definition which is satisfactory even to themselves. But whatever definition may be accepted, it is certain that in the Bible we have some of the finest examples of what all will agree to be poetry of a high order. Most readers of the Bible have to judge of it, as most readers of the poetry of Homer and Virgil judge of their works, though a translation. David and Isaiah thus suffer; but even when so studied, the glowing lyrics of the one and the seraphic prophecies of the other, place them in the front rank of the writers of all countries and centuries. The poetry of the Bible is unsurpassed in loftiness of thought and eloquence of expression. This poetry is animated by the breath of God; it is aglow with the soul of the Eternal. At the same time it throbs with all human sympathies; it sings in our gladness, weeps in our sadness, mourns in our defeats, and shouts in our triumphs. It is equally at home in funeral obsequies and at marriage festivities. It belongs exclusively to no school of poetry; it possesses many of the excellences of all schools of noblest song. It belongs to the nineteenth century as truly as to the remotest past; and it will be equally appropriate to the thought and life of the most distant future. Milton declared that the Greek and Roman classics are unworthy to be compared with Zion's songs; and Sir Daniel Sanford says that, "In lyric flow and fire, in crushing force, in majesty that seems still to echo the awful sounds once heard beneath the thunderclouds of Mount Sinai, the poetry of the ancient Scriptures is the most superb that ever burned within the breast of man."

Did you ever read the book of Job at a single sitting? If not, I take the liberty of suggesting that you do so at the very first opportunity. I have recently made the experiment and I am the better prepared to appreciate what Carlyle says when, apart from all theories about it, he calls it one of the grandest things ever written with pen, and then adds: "Sublime sorrow, sublime reconciliation; oldest choral melody as of the heart of mankind; so soft and great as the summer midnight, as the world with its seas and stars! There is nothing written, I think, in the Bible, or out of it, of equal literary merit."

The Hebrew bard was, under the inspiration of God, a law unto himself. He stood with uncovered head and upturned face to listen to God before he began to sing to men. He stood in the immediate presence of God; he felt God's touch and heard God's voice. Then his own voice was tuned and then the hearts of men were touched. He followed no human authority; he studied in no earthly school. He had no earthly teachers; he was God's child, singing the song his Father taught him. It is true that he sang no great epic, as did Homer, Virgil, and Milton;

and it is true that he wrote no great continuous drama, as did Shakespeare, although in the Songs of Solomon and in the book of Job there are elements of true dramatic literature; but in lyric poetry, the poetry of the heart, he sings as never man sang before nor since. The echoes of those songs, first sung in harvestfield or battlefield, or amid "the munitions of rocks," or on vine-clad hillsides, have echoed through the world, and will continue to be heard until the redeemed come to Zion with still sweeter songs of gladness and triumph.

II. INDIRECT INFLUENCE. The indirect influence of the Bible on literature is worthy of consideration. It has ennobled every language into which it has been translated. Its thoughts are so lofty that the moment they are embodied in human speech, whatever that speech may be, it is exalted, purified, and glorified. When it came into the Greek and Latin languages it largely regenerated even the vehicle which communicated its thought. It necessitated the creation of new words; and it gave new and noble meanings to old words. It is not too much to say that it almost created a new Greek and Latin tongue. It has given noble themes and thoughts to our greatest writers. Go through a library and count the number of the books which the Bible has suggested. You will at once put into the category, Dante's "Divine Comedy," Tasso's "Jerusalem Delivered," Spenser's "Faerie Queene," Milton's "Paradise Lost" and "Paradise Regained," Pollok's "Course of Time," Pope's "Messiah," and many others of like character. It has often given the idea of the characters which are the subjects of many books; in this way, we are indebted to it for striking features in Scott's "Ivanhoe," Mrs. Stowe's "Uncle Tom's Cabin," and for many characters in George Eliot, in Tennyson, in Byron, in Shakespeare, and in many other writers. It is said that the Red Cross Knight, in Spenser's "Faerie Queene," is but Paul's armed Christian in the sixth chapter of the Epistle to the Ephesians; that Pope's "Messiah" is but a paraphrase of prophetic and seraphic passages in Isaiah; that the noblest strains in Cowper's "Task" drew their inspiration and part of their imagery from the same rapt prophet; that the "Thanatopsis" of Bryant is but the expansion of a passage in Job; that Wordsworth's "Ode on Immortality" could never have been written but for Paul's fifteenth chapter of First Corinthians and the eighth chapter of Romans; that Shakespeare's conception of woman, of a Desdemona and of an Ophelia, would have been impossible, had not his mind been permeated by a Bible ideal. This suggestive thought could be much expanded, and these instructive illustrations might be greatly multiplied. The Bible gave all these men—working in different departments of genius—their inspiration. Shall we be so inconsistent as to rejoice in the streams while we despise the fountain whence they flowed? The Bible is a light to the path and the lamp to the feet of the noblest literature. No man may claim the honors of the highest culture if he is ignorant of the word of God. Let it sing itself through the soul, giving clearness to the thought, wings to the imagination, enterprise in practical life, inspiration to daily duty, hope in death, and glory in eternity!

III. THE BIBLE AND THE FINE ARTS. It is fitting also that I call your attention to the influence of the Bible on the fine arts. This thought I have somewhat touched, but it is worthy of fuller development. In no department of human genius is its presence more marked. It abounds in appeals to the finer sensibilities, and it arouses the noblest æsthetic elements in our nature. It throbs with human sympathy, and it is in touch everywhere with nature. It has been truly said that there is more of nature in the book of Psalms than in all the writings of the Greek and the Latin poets. It will readily be admitted that great Greek sculptors lived and won enduring fame without the direct teachings of the Bible; but it ought also to be acknowledged that the sculpture which is inspired by the Bible contains loftier conceptions and makes stronger appeals to our nobler natures, than do the works of those earlier sculptors. They found their chief employment in illustrating physical perfection and beauty; but Christian sculptors incarnate spiritual and divine thoughts. But for the Bible, Angelo's "Moses," Canova's "Repentant Magdalen," and Thorwaldsen's "Christ and the Apostles," would have been impossible. But for the Bible, Raphael's "Transfiguration" never would have been conceived. When Raphael would perpetuate his name to unborn generations he must ascend "the holy mount," stand in the supernal glory, and gaze on the transfigured Christ. As the "Transfiguration" was his greatest, so it was his last work. He died in early manhood, with the "Transfiguration" on his heart and brain. That picture was carried in the funeral procession to his grave. To the Bible we are indebted for Angelo's "Last Judgment," Da Vinci's "Last Supper," Correggio's "Nativity," for the works of Titian, Holman Hunt, Doré, and many others.

To the Bible we are indebted for the noblest music of the world.

> Devotion borrows music's tone,
>   And music takes devotion's wing,
> And like the bird that hails the sun
>   They soar to heaven, and soaring sing.

The songs of the day are for the day; but the music that endures is religious music. The

Ambrosian and Gregorian chants are the echoes of Bible songs. When Handel was discouraged by attempting to give opera in a foreign language, he accepted an invitation from several notables of Ireland to visit Dublin. From a friend he received a text from the Bible on which he composed his immortal work, known at the first as the "Sacred Oratorio," known now as the "Messiah." Both in Dublin and in London this work gave him immediate fame; and it has since crowned him throughout the world with unfading glory. The debt which music, painting, sculpture, and literature owe to the Bible cannot be fully estimated. The Bible gave us the "Creation" of Haydn, the works of Mozart, of Mendelssohn, and of Beethoven, and the grand chorals of Bach, and the works of all the great musicians the world has yet produced. It has been well said that Haydn has not exhausted the wonders of creation, nor Handel the glories of the Messiah; and there is vastly more music yet in the Bible than has ever yet been heard by the children of men.

IV. INFLUENCE ON LEGISLATION. The influence of the Bible on legislation is equally important with its power over music. The great principles taught in the Bible are those needed in all the relations of life to this hour. Great problems in legislation are yet unsolved, and great difficulties now confront all legislators.

He was truly a wise leader of men who said, "Nothing is politically right which is morally wrong." The principles of God's word should prevail alike in the counting-room of merchandise and in the halls of legislation. The teachings of the books of Moses are to be studied by the student of medicine as truly as by those who make and execute the laws of the land. At a recent convention of medical men, held in the city of Boston, a brilliant physician of New York City affirmed in an able paper that in many important respects the medical science of to-day is not up to the sanitary code given in the law of Moses. Whence had Moses this marvelous wisdom? Questions affecting the relations of the rich and the poor, the tenure of property and the rights of man, are now demanding answers. The spirit of the Bible alone furnishes the solutions to the perplexing problems. In its teachings are found the true "Liberty, equality, and fraternity," of which socialists have dreamed. With great clearness and beauty it declares, in substance, that whether a man be black or white, red or yellow, rich or poor,

> A man's a man for a' that.

Moses was the greatest legislator of the world. The laws of all civilized countries rest to-day upon the Ten Commandments; in them we have the germ of all moral duty. No man who has ever lived has exercised so extensive and powerful an influence on the race as Moses, the leader and lawgiver of the Hebrew people. The Bible is the cradle of all true civil and religious liberty. Egypt and Phœnicia borrowed from its light; so indirectly did Greece; Rome borrowed from Greece, and the laws of Rome are the basis of the codes of Europe and America. A distinguished French jurist, himself an atheist, in comparing the laws of Moses with those of other great lawgivers says: "Lycurgus wrote, not for the people, but for an army; it was a barrack he erected, not a commonwealth; and sacrificing everything to the military spirit, he mutilated human nature to crush it into armor. Solon could not resist the effeminate and relaxing influence of Athens. In Moses alone do we find a morality distinct from policy, and for all times and peoples. The trumpet of Sinai still finds an echo in the conscience of mankind, the Decalogue still binds us all." Disraeli says in his "Tancred": "The life and prosperity of England are protected by the laws of Sinai. The hardworking people of England are secured a day of rest in every week by the laws of Sinai." The same author again says: "As an exponent of the human heart, as a soother of the troubled spirit, to whose harp do the people of England fly for sympathy and solace? Is it to Byron, or Wordsworth, or even the myriad-minded Shakespeare?

No. The most popular poet in England is the sweet singer of Israel, and by no other race except his own have his odes been so often sung. It was the sword of the Lord and of Gideon that won for England her boasted liberties; and the Scotch achieved their religious freedom, chanting upon their hillsides the same canticles which cheered the heart of Judah amid their glens."

Blessed Bible! It is the flower of all the world's books; it is the softest pillow for the aching head; it is the best balm for the broken heart; it brings heaven down to earth; it lifts earth up to heaven.

Many men have entered the arena to tilt against Moses and the Pentateuch. It is well for many of them that Moses has been long dead. Those who opposed him in the courts of Pharaoh, or as a soldier when he drove back his enemies to the swamp-girdled city of Meroe, found him to be a foeman worthy of their steel. Moses will live when all his critics are utterly forgotten. Pharaoh strove against him, and he sank like lead into the Red Sea. Jannes and Jambres, the Egyptian magicians, "withstood Moses," and they are named only to show their defeat and humiliation. "The grass" of merely destructive criticism "withereth, the flower" of infidel oratory "fadeth; but the word of our God shall stand forever."

V. THE BIBLE'S MORAL STANDARD. But, in the last place, I commend the study of the Bible because it places before us the highest standard of moral living to be found in literature. In it are hid all the treasures of wisdom and knowledge. When Sir Walter Scott lay dying he asked his son-in-law, Mr. Lockhart, to read for him. "What book?" said Mr. Lockhart. "What book?" said Sir Walter; "there is but one book—the Bible—read that." He who had read so widely, and had contributed so many immortal pages to literature, gives this testimony to the value of the Bible. Charles Dickens was in the habit of urging his children never to neglect the reading of the Bible, as it contained the highest rules of morality known among men. The Bible is the true friend of civil and religious liberty. Where the Bible is practically unknown, as in Spain and Cuba, there religious liberty is virtually unknown. The Bible condemns all oppression and inspires all worthy national and personal character. The men who won civil and religious liberty for Britain and America were men who believed in God and in his holy book. The Bible sweetens all domestic life, and is the savor of life in all social relations. It glorifies marriage, beautifies home, and prophesies of heaven. It transforms a house into a home; it makes earth the foretaste of paradise. It makes the wilderness of social life glad, and it makes the desert of earth blossom into the garden of God. Let us love the holy book, that it may fully control our daily lives for the good of man and the glory of God. Most of all, let all men believe in the divine Lord and Saviour who is in the fullest sense the divine Word, whom this book makes known. Then, under the influence of this highest Word of God,

     Shall all men's good
  Be each man's rule, and universal peace
  Lie like a shaft of light across the land,
  And like a lane of beams athwart the sea,
  Thro' all the circle of the golden year.

II

THE FRUITFUL WORD

"For as the rain cometh down, and the snow from heaven, and returneth not thither, but watereth the earth, and maketh it bring forth and bud, that it may give seed to the sower, and bread to the eater: So shall my word be that goeth forth out of my mouth: it shall not return unto me void, but it shall accomplish that which I please, and it shall prosper in the thing whereto I sent it." Isa. 55: 10, 11.

II

STANDING one day during the past week, watching the rain falling in copious showers, this beautiful passage of Scripture kept singing itself in my soul. The falling rain was a striking commentary on the inspired word. The book of nature and the book of revelation are not two books, but one; they are simply different sections of the one great volume by the one divine Author. Scientists on the one hand, and theologians on the other, make a great mistake when they represent the teachings of nature as being in opposition to the teachings of revelation. The apparent contradiction occasionally seen is in the incorrect interpretations of these teachings, and not in the teachings themselves. God has not one law for nature and another for grace—not one law for the natural world and another for the spiritual world. One law permeates the entire universe. The nineteenth Psalm beautifully illustrates the divine harmony between nature and revelation.

It shows that revealed truth is superior to the light of nature. Nature shows God's hand; revelation God's heart. Nature is the gray dawn of the morning; revelation is the splendor of the noonday sun. In this psalm no attempt is made to disparage the value of truth revealed by nature. The first six verses show how the divine perfections are illustrated by the works of creation; but when we come to the seventh verse we feel that brighter light is thrown upon the works of God's hands, and a firmer foundation is placed beneath our own feet. "The law of the Lord" is placed in strong contrast with the works of God in creation. But both belong to the same system of religion; both are designed to illustrate the power, wisdom, and love of him who is the framer of all worlds and the Father of all spirits. Every true disciple ought to rejoice in the teachings of nature as truly, though not so fully, as in the teachings of the Bible.

We have here in the first six verses, the voice of nature; in the next six, the voice of revelation; and in the last two verses, the voice of the regenerated child supplicating his Heavenly Father. A true Christian ought not to allow the mere secular scholar to rob him of his Father's voice in creation. Within the past few years attention has been given as never before to the relation between the teachings of these two great volumes. Dr. Hugh Macmillan, of Scotland, has shown how much of nature there is in the Bible; with equal scientific knowledge and religious reverence, he has traced the frequent allusions to plant and vine, to herb and tree, to times and seasons, and, indeed, to the wide range of nature found in the Bible, as illustrations of divine truths. This is a vast department of profitable inquiry; it has been thus far but very imperfectly examined by scholars competent alike by scientific and biblical knowledge. Enough, however, has been done to show the great possibilities yet to be discovered in this line of natural and biblical study. Inspired writers lived in such loving sympathy with nature that they were her children and disciples, and so they constantly illustrated religious truths by reference to earth and air, sea and sky. The Prophet Isaiah, in using the striking figure found in this text, is following the usual method of Bible writers.

We shall not make any distinction between the rain and the snow, as they practically are one in this passage. By God's word here we might understand every word that goeth forth out of his mouth, whenever, wherever, and however spoken; but we understand especially the Scriptures of the Old and the New Testaments as they have been given by holy men writing under the inspiration of God.

1. God's word and the rain are alike in the variety of their sources. Both come partly from above and partly from below. It is conceivable that God should supply wells and streams by

drawing water from the oceans without causing it to ascend to the clouds and then to fall upon the earth; but for wise purposes this latter method is employed. The rain, therefore, comes as we observe it from above. Not less so does the divine word. It bears the sign-manual of God himself. The Bible must ever remain the Book of books. As the Bible comes from God, so it leads to God. The inspired writers stood in the audience chamber of the King, and the messages thus received they imparted. No man need fear for the permanency and the authority of the word of God; it is its own witness. It comes to us with the tone and authority of its divine Author. Its seraphic poetry, its rapt prophecy, its calm logic, its practical doctrine, and all its truths throb with the life, sparkle with the radiancy, and glow with the love of God, their Author and our Creator and Redeemer.

But both the rain and the word have an earthly source as well as an heavenly. From sea and lake, from bay and river, the rain goes up in vapors before it comes down in showers. It comes down, but it also goes up; it is of heaven, but it is also of the earth. There is the mingling of both elements in the descending shower. Not less so is there this mingling in the divine word. Many have spoken of the human element in the Bible as if it were a defect in divine revelation. But their criticisms show how utterly they have misunderstood the purpose and method of divine revelation.

If God is to communicate his thought to men, it is fitting that men should be the channel through which the truth should flow. If he were communicating his thought to angels or seraphs, some angelic or seraphic medium might fittingly be chosen. It would be useless to make a revelation to men which men could not understand. Such a revelation must come through human channels and be adapted to human needs. The human element in the Bible, therefore, so far from detracting from its value, is one of its chief glories. The glory of an art, discovery, or attainment of whatever kind, is that it accomplishes the purpose of its existence. If the Bible is a revelation of divine truth to men, it must so come to men that they can understand its teaching and thereby be brought into obedience to its Author. We thank God for the human element in the Bible. Its presence is a proof of God's wisdom and condescension. The incarnate Word, Jesus Christ, was human as truly he was divine. He took not upon him the nature of angels, but the seed of Abraham. He inserted himself into our race at its lowest and weakest point. The human element in the incarnate Word gave completion and perfection to Jesus Christ as the Saviour of lost men. The Son of

God, he was as truly the Son of man; the Son of God, he was as truly the Son of Mary; the Ancient of days, he was also the Child of the manger. Of heaven and heavenly, the incarnate Word and the revealed word are both, in a real sense, of the earth and earthly, even as is the rain. The human element in Christ, or rather the divine element under a human form, and with human attributes and affections, is what the theologians call anthropomorphism. The presence of this earthly element is no ground for criticism, but is rather a cause for gratitude and joy.

2. Both the rain and the word are alike also in the nature of their supplies. The earth without rain is barren and sterile; the hearts of men without the dews of heavenly grace are equally barren and sterile. In meeting the wants of the earth and of human hearts both the rain and the word silently give their supplies. We are constantly impressed with the fact that most of the great movements of God, both in creation and in redemption, give out no sound. Religion is a more pervasive, dominant, and beneficent force than either its friends or its foes ordinarily appreciate. Like many other mighty forces, it works largely in silence. It does not give out a loud report when it undermines some hoary error or establishes some benignant truth. God's great heavens and his vast laboratory in the

earth give forth, for the most part, no sound in their gigantic movements. God's greatest works move in silent realms. Christianity is no exception to this law. Like its Founder, it comes not with observation. Heathen thinkers and writers of the early centuries of Christianity were strangely ignorant of its power, and apparently even of its presence. Their silence is surprising; it is almost unaccountable. In the meantime, Christianity was leavening literature, philosophy, art, government, and social life; it was the force hidden in the very heart of society, which was to some degree to affect the whole Roman world. But even in our own day many men are strangely thoughtless as to the place and power of Christianity among the roborant forces of modern life.

Its predominance and beneficence, like the majesty and glory of the sun, are even with many Christians matters of course. Some who are the foes of Christianity do not, because they will not, recognize its influence at its full value. It was prophesied of its divine Founder, that he should "not cry, nor lift up, nor cause his voice to be heard in the street." The sun moves in silence from the rising to the setting of the same; but his power is immeasurable. The great dome of the noble capitol at Washington moves daily through a considerable space when the sun breathes upon it from its fiery heart. All the great iron bridges and other iron structures throb with life and expand with uncontrollable power when kissed by the sun. The law of gravitation permeates the universe silently as the falling dew, but mighty as the rushing storm. God's great forces are at work in the laboratory of nature at each springtime, covering the earth with greenness, decking it with flowers, and clothing the trees in their summer garb, but giving forth no sound in the midst of these gigantic processes. God's sublimest achievements are wrought in seclusion and silence. More water goes up in the hour of a summer noon by the silent attraction of the sun than could be pumped into the heavens by the noisy machinery of men working continuously through generations. I saw a few days ago a rock which had been rent in twain by a plant which grew in one of its seams. A seed, dropped perhaps by a bird, continued to grow until it split the great rock into fragments. A vine grew in the tower of an historic castle and would have thrown it to the earth had not the vine been cut.

Life everywhere is as majestic in its movements as it is mysterious in its origin. The Czar Nicholas, observing the unusual thoughtfulness of his son Alexander, asked him its cause. The reply was: "I am thinking about the wretched condition of the serfs, and if ever I become czar I will give them their freedom."

The words of the boy troubled the heart of the czar. It was hoped that the influence of the palace would remove such strange thoughts from the heart of the youth. The explanation of his anxiety was that while reading the Bible he learned that all men were brothers, and if brothers the czar could not hold them as serfs. A seed of God's word had fallen into this young boy's heart, and it was soon to bring forth fruit in the liberty of millions of serfs. Amid the defeats of the Crimean War, Nicholas died of a broken heart, and Alexander II. became the czar of all the Russias. At once he began to mature plans for the liberation of the serfs and, although he availed himself of the counsels of his own statesmen and of philanthropists from other countries, the credit of maturing the plans and issuing the imperial ukase, which translated a nation of serfs out of slavery into liberty, was due to Alexander himself. Two years before the illustrious Lincoln wrote his Emancipation Proclamation, the immortal Alexander issued his liberating ukase. The two great liberators fell by the hands of assassins; but side by side they abide in the niche of fame crowned with unfading glory. The teachings of God's word, illustrated by the spirit of Jesus Christ, destroyed slavery in Russia and in America; and the real hand that wrote these emancipating proclamations bore in its palm the print of a nail. True Christianity and not atheism is the benefactor of the race; true Christianity levels the race—levels it not down, but up, giving dignity to the lowly and gentleness to the lofty.

The rain and the word are alike also in the abundance of their supplies. Many think that lately we have been having too much rain; but in that respect, as in regard to every earthly occurrence, God's way is better than ours. One sometimes wonders why so large a portion of the world is covered by water. One contemplates such vast rivers as the Amazon, Volga, Dneiper, and Nile, and the great rivers of our own republic, with mingled wonder and admiration. For more than three thousand miles the Nile flows, constantly distributing blessings in its course; and for nearly one thousand five hundred miles of this distance it receives no tributary. It moves on in its majesty, transforming what would otherwise be barren wastes into fruitful fields. The abundance of blessings which the word of God brings is still more worthy of adoring wonder and constant gratitude. His word is never spoken in vain; it never returns to God void. The rain often falls upon barren rocks and arid sands, and to our thought its abundance is in vain; but God has a design in every drop that falls, whether on barren deserts or on fertile fields. Not less has he a design in regard to the preaching of the word. Even when it seems to be despised and rejected by the proud, the sensual, and the unbelieving, he is accomplishing his purpose. The abundance of the offered blessing takes from men every excuse for their rejection; the very abundance often leads to acceptance of the truth which at first was rejected.

There is harmony also in the impartiality of the bestowment of the rain and the word. Both come alike on the just and the unjust. God's proffers of mercy are made to all classes and conditions of men. But there is a solemn woe pronounced upon those who receive blessings from God and who do not use them aright. We are taught that "the earth which drinketh in the rain that cometh oft upon it, and bringeth forth herbs meet for them by whom it is dressed, receiveth blessing from God; but that which beareth thorns and briers is rejected, and is nigh unto cursing, whose end is to be burned." It is an unspeakably solemn thing to receive rich blessings from God and fail to use them for our good and for his glory.

3. There is a close relation also in their effects between the rain and the word. Both the rain and the word are refreshing. Flowers and plants, animals and men, long for and rejoice in the refreshment which the rain bestows. The word of God, as truly as the rain, refreshes the weary and inspires the faint. Finely has the thought of the psalmist been expressed as he describes the

refreshment which God's ancient people received in their wilderness journey:

> O God, thou to thy people
>   Didst send a plenteous rain,
> Thy heritage when weary,
>   Thou didst refresh again.

Many of God's children to-day can bear similar testimony to the blessed influence of God's truth upon their hearts. It has revived their drooping faith, encouraged their fainting hope, and quickened their flagging zeal. While at times this spiritual rain may have fallen upon their hearts, producing as little effect as the natural rain upon the deserts of Arabia or of Africa, at other times their souls have opened to receive it, as plants to receive the natural rain, and they have been refreshed and quickened, even as the flowers and plants of the earth.

Another effect which both the rain and the word produce is in their *cleansing power*. But for the copious showers of rain the streets of this great city would be still greater causes of discomfort to the eye and of danger to the health. We are often far more dependent upon the showers of rain for the measure of cleanliness which we have in our streets than upon the entire street-cleaning department. The Augean stables of classic story fitly represent the condition of some of our streets, and the stream of water flowing through those stables suggests the value of the showers which cleanse our streets. Not less, but more cleansing is the word of God when received into good and honest hearts. When Dr. Johnson was asked by a young man to give advice regarding reading, he said : "Give days and nights to the study of Addison if you would be master of the English tongue, or what is more worth, an honest man." If the writings of uninspired men could produce this effect, how much more the words of the living God. The psalmist, in answer to the question, "Wherewithal shall a young man cleanse his way?" answered, "By taking heed thereto according to thy word." Elsewhere he said : "Thy word have I hid in mine heart that I might not sin against thee." And the Apostle Paul uses these very suggestive words, "Christ also loved the church, and gave himself for it that he might sanctify and cleanse it with the washing of water by the word." And a greater than the apostle or the psalmist said : " Now ye are clean through the word which I have spoken unto you." Come, O stream, O living stream, O crystal stream, O golden stream, flowing from the throne and heart of God, and cleanse our hearts until they shall be as wool, until they shall be whiter than snow.

Still another effect in which the rain and the word are alike is in their *fertilizing power.* All that parts of the Sahara Desert need to make them abundantly fruitful is a sufficient supply of water. Wherever an artesian well has been sunk, there an oasis has been created. All that is needed on some of our Western plains is the stream of water which irrigation brings. When Elijah's prayer opened the windows of heaven and the rain came in copious showers, the famine ceased and plenty was restored. It is evermore true that when "the heaven gave rain," then "the earth brought forth her fruit." The husbandman has no hope for the fruits of the earth until the early and latter rains fall. Equally true is it in the spiritual life. Only as God's doctrine drops as the rain, and as his speech distills like the dew, or the small rain, or as the showers upon the grass, will men and women bring forth fruit unto holiness. When God visits the church and waters it, then will its own banks overflow, and the spreading blessing will give joy to unnumbered souls. Perhaps there is no period of British history so marked by blessing as the reigns of Elizabeth and Victoria. Hume relates that when Elizabeth was passing through the streets of London to her coronation, a boy who personated Truth was let down through one of the triumphal arches and presented to her a copy of the Bible. She received the book with many expressions of joy, pressed it to her heart, and declared that of all the costly testimonies which the city had given her that day this present was by far the most precious. We are all familiar with the request made by a thoughtful African prince to Queen Victoria, to know by what means her kingdom had been raised to so great a height of grandeur, and we are also familiar with the answer which, it is said, she gave in the shape of a copy of the holy Scriptures, saying to the ambassador: "Tell your master that in this book is hidden the secret of English greatness." Whether or not this incident be historically accurate, the fact remains that the teachings of the Bible are truly the secret of Britain's power throughout the world.

We learn from this comparison that God's word is to be received with gratitude. Every thoughtful man knows that it is as necessary to the growth of the spiritual life as rain is to the growth of vegetable life. The man who makes light of God's word takes unnecessary pains to advertise his ignorance and his folly. Jesus Christ is God's Word in the largest and noblest sense. He is God's unspeakable gift to lost men. How are we treating this gift? Have we received Jesus Christ into our hearts? We cannot remain unmoved by the knowledge of this gift. We must either accept or reject this blessing.

We also learn that we ought to feel our dependence on God's word. Has God spoken?

His voice should be the end of all controversy. Let us not forget that we are at the last to be judged by the word of our God. When we stand at the judgment bar, the book of nature, the book of providence, and especially the book of revelation, will be opened, and we shall be judged according to the records and principles of these books. We ought also to have perfect assurance that God's word shall not return unto him void. It is the declaration of his will. The promises shall have their full accomplishment, and not one jot or tittle shall fail. God's precious promises of mercy we ought to believe; his words of rebuke we should heed, and his threatenings we should fear. His warnings are as much a message of his love as are his promises. May he to-day plant in our hearts the imperishable seed of his word; may it be watered by the dews of his heavenly grace, and may this seed bring forth fruit, some thirty, some sixty, and some an hundred-fold in this life, and in the world to come life everlasting!

III

THE RESISTLESS WEAPON

"*For the word of God is quick, and powerful, and sharper than any twoedged sword, piercing even to the dividing asunder of soul and spirit, and of the joints and marrow, and is a discerner of the thoughts and intents of the heart.*" Heb. 4 : 12.

III

THE Bible is now in the furnace of trial, and the furnace is heated seven times hotter than it is wont to be heated. We have no fear, however, for the divine word. The Bible is quite used to harsh treatment. In the minds of its hostile critics, it has been overthrown so often that their judgment is not to be taken as conclusive in this regard. Some one has said that the Bible is a cube, and so is always of the same height, however often it may be overturned. The intellectual giants in the past attempted in vain to destroy the truth of God; the pigmies of the present will certainly not accomplish what the giants failed to achieve. It is interesting, amid the Babel of modern criticism, to know what inspired writers thought and said of the inspired word. We have in this text an admirable statement of a Bible writer's opinion of the Bible, to whose perfection under the divine Spirit he was contributing his part. What does the Bible think of itself? We have heard what the critics think of Moses and Isaiah. It would be instructive to know what Moses and Isaiah think of their critics. It is certain that when Moses was living, neither in Pharaoh's palace nor on the field of battle, were men ready to attack him. If he were now living some of his critics might be more modest in their assertions and less forward in their attacks.

Mere destructive criticism is worthy of but little respect. In no other sphere can the minimum of talent so certainly secure the maximum of notice. A child or an idiot with a knife or a hammer, let loose in a gallery of paintings or a hall of statuary, can destroy more in an hour than Angelo or Raphael could create in a lifetime. Destructive criticism requires but little ability and has equally little utility. At times it may have a brief mission. It may awaken curiosity; it may evoke inquiry. Many a minister can attract no attention by earnestly expounding the gospel; but the same man by attacking the gospel and denouncing recognized beliefs, will have a brief notoriety in the secular and religious press. By once hurling a hymn book from their pulpits at the windows of the church, some pastors would attract more notice than by their ordinary preaching for a score of years. But mere destruction is unworthy the ambition of a noble man and the attainments of a broad scholar. God often overrules destructive work, however, for the establishment of his truth. The opposition of Porphyry in his day called into the arena many defenders of Christ and his gospel. The attacks upon Christianity in our day have only served to show the solidity of its deep foundations. Let no believer be alarmed; let no one feel obliged to steady the ark of God; it is certain that God will take care of his word and his work. The business of the pulpit is to preach the truth and not to apologize for God and the Bible. A pastor is engaged in a sorry labor when he is simply unsettling the beliefs of men, and robbing the Bible of its authority and beauty. A man of this character may have some sphere of usefulness, but it is certainly not in the pulpit or church of God.

Whoever the author of the Epistle to the Hebrews was, he had an exalted conception of the character and influence of the word of God; and that conception he has expressed in language as beautiful as it is forceful, and as lofty in its rhetoric as it is logical in its reasoning. His purpose in this text is to show that God knows every act of our lives and every thought of our hearts. All forms of untruthfulness, insincerity, and hypocrisy, we are here taught, will be exposed to God's piercing sight. It is impossible for men to deceive the Almighty. His gaze is all-penetrating; his knowledge goes to the bottom of the soul; he will uncover men to themselves and to the sight of an assembled universe. Only as our sins are covered by the righteousness of Christ, or washed away in his precious blood, can they be hidden from the sight of God. His omniscience is a truth as sublime as it is solemn.

What are we to understand by the phrase "the word of God" in the text? Does it mean the threatening referred to in the previous verse? So some have said. Does it mean the gospel as a whole? So some have said. Does it mean the whole range of divine revelation? Does it mean the Lord Jesus, the essential and eternal Word? Although this title is not given to him in this connection, he is in the highest, the fullest, and the divinest sense the Word of God. The meaning here will include all these truths. The word of God is whatever God has spoken, whether in promise or prophecy, whether in threatening or in doctrine. God's truth goes to the depths of the soul; it uncovers the secrets of every life. What are the characteristics of this word as here given?

The first characteristic named is that it is *quick*. This word is a translation of a Greek word which literally means "living." This now almost obsolete Saxon word "quick" retains its natural meaning in the expression, "cut to the quick," and in similar uses still current in daily speech. It suggests here that the word of God is alive with vital energy. This characteristic certainly belongs to the word of God. It is living in itself, and not cold, formal, and dead. It is the active, energetic, and living truth which God evermore speaks. Speech is sacred; speech possesses individuality; language is a living original; language grows and is not made; speech is immortal. Humboldt considers language not as a dead product, but as an animate creature. He affirms that man is differentiated from the animal kingdom by the faculty of speech. Men and God alike use words. Language stands related to thought as the body does to the soul. There is a moral quality in words. There never can be pure speech except it come from a pure heart. Language wraps up histories and prophecies. Language gives us fossil poetry and verbal ethics. If these things be true of human speech, how much more significant is the speech of the Almighty! Not only are God's words quick, but they are quickening; they are not only living, but they give life. The word of the living God is a living and enlivening word. His word lives forevermore. Whatever may die, the word of God must live. His truth is possessed of an immortal life. All other literature may perish, but God's word shall endure for evermore. "All flesh is grass, and all the goodliness thereof is as the flower of the field. The grass withereth, the flower fadeth; but the word of our God shall stand for ever."

We learn also that the word of God is *powerful:* that it is energetic, instinct with force. It lays bare the secret feelings of the heart; it awakens the fears of the most careless of men; it sternly arouses the conscience; and at times it lifts up its voice until the awful scenes of the judgment day pass in review before the eyes of guilty men. It causes the sinner to see the great white throne and to hear the awful words of the eternal Judge. God's truth is now controlling all the great events in the political and moral world. God's word is girdling the world. His truth makes thrones tremble and totter; it makes tyrants quake and fear; it gives freedom to the slave, and makes earth a training school for heaven. Believe me, men and women, when the Spirit of God takes the sword of the Spirit, which is the word of God, then that word is powerful to convict sinners, to convert penitents, and to comfort saints. It is so powerful that it can pull down the strongholds of sin; that it can make the lame to walk, the deaf to hear, the dumb to sing, the blind to see, and the dead to live. The hammer of God's truth can break in pieces the most flinty heart; it can shatter the refuges of lies behind which men seek protection; it can batter down the walls of Satan's kingdom, and on the ruins thereof erect the everlasting kingdom of God's dear Son. This word comes down as the rain and snow from heaven, but returns not thither. It never goes forth out of God's mouth in vain; it ever accomplishes that which he pleases and prospers in the thing whereunto he hath sent it. When Christ spoke one word the centurion's servant was healed. God's word hath penetrating, healing, illumining, and illimitable power to-day. Let us believe in the omnipotence of divine truth; let us possess our souls in patience. God will magnify his word above all his name.

The third characteristic is thus stated— *Sharper than any twoedged sword.* Commentators call attention to the fact that the word translated two-edged literally means a two-mouthed sword. It is easy to understand how this idea is associated with the word sword; the sword is thought of as devouring all before it, and thus its edge comes to be spoken of as a mouth. The sword was conceived of as a terrible beast which destroyed all antagonists. The power of God's word is thus set forth by this striking figure. Similar language is elsewhere used in Scripture concerning the word of God. In Isa. 49 : 2 we read, " He hath made my mouth like a sharp sword "; and in Rev. 1 : 16, " Out of his mouth went a sharp twoedged sword." Similar language is found in still other portions of the Bible regarding the penetrating and irresistible power of God's word. It cuts both ways; it enters where no other sword can enter; it dissects as is not possible in the case of any other instrument. It will cut the hand of the man who uses it unskillfully, and it is a dangerous weapon to have used against us. By this word we are to be judged, and by it justified or condemned. If it be on our side, no weapon formed by man can prosper against us; if it be against us, no weapon formed by man can protect us. What the two-edged Roman sword did to the bodies of the foes of Rome that this sword does to the foes of Jesus Christ and his kingdom, "piercing even to the dividing asunder of soul and spirit, and of the joints and marrow." God's word will go straight to the heart, to the very center of motive and action.

When soul is distinguished from spirit as here, we understand by the former word the lower faculty, while by spirit a superior power. The word soul means the animal life as distinguished from the immortal life; the word spirit refers to the immaterial and immortal element in our complex being. We have in Scripture the three-fold classification, "your whole spirit, soul, and body," and this distinction we now make. These three are mysteriously united in life, and to separate them is surely to cause death. The word of God, the sword of the Spirit, penetrates the very heart of the sinner and slays him. The Apostle Paul tells us that when the commandment came sin revived and he died; the law slew him; he was cut down under conviction, and fell pierced to the heart, and lay dying at Jesus' feet. The figure of the sword is still retained in the text, and it is represented as reaching the joints and marrow and as discerning the thoughts and intents of the heart. It seems to dismember the body, cutting through the bones to the marrow. God's truth will uncover every hypocrite. It enters irresistibly into the soul. Some have supposed that the apostle was arguing from some tremendous punishment which came upon the ancient Israelites, that he is speaking of the word of God as producing effects like lightning or fire from heaven.

Not only does this wonderful word discern the thoughts, but it reaches even to the half-formed intentions of the soul. It strikes below the sphere of our conscious thoughts into the realm of half-formed intentions, and we are judged in the sight of God according to our character and purposes. Many men have been conscious of this property of God's word. When it has been faithfully preached, and they have been deeply convicted, they have often charged the preacher with having knowledge of the most private events in their lives. Some have supposed that their neighbors gave information to the preacher. Frequently in my own ministry have I had experience of the power of God's word in these respects. These results were due to the energy of the divine Spirit using the holy word as its two-mouthed sword. Every earnest gospel ministry has witnessed similar effects from the faithful declaration of God's truth. God's word is a hammer and a sword; and the preacher needs skill and strength for its right use. The hammer will not break the rock in pieces nor the sword pierce to the joints and marrow unless both hammer and sword are directed by a trained hand, a skillful mind, and a consecrated heart. God help us to know how aright to use these divine instruments! Wonderful language is here employed. When a man is so pierced by this sword he dies. Oh, blessed truth! Oh, divine sword! God grant that the slain of the Lord may be many this day! God grant that the divine breath may then come to the slain, that they may live as a great army of witnesses and soldiers for God!

The last characteristic of the word of God is that it *is a discerner of the thoughts and intents of the heart.* This thought I have already touched upon, but it is worthy of fuller presentation. Here the word is represented as going through the chambers of the soul as with a lighted candle, or, more strictly speaking, the thoughts and intents of the heart come forth into conspicuous view by the word of God. God's truths reveal men to themselves in their true character; it brings to light their forgotten sins. They see themselves more nearly as God sees them; and their motives now appear in all their sinfulness. Evils whose presence they did not suspect are now seen in all their vileness. God's word floods their souls with its heavenly light, and men are then startled at the Satanic hostility to God which they discover in their own hearts. All purposes, all deepest thoughts, all vilest imaginations, lie naked and opened to the eyes of God. The Greek word "opened" in the next verse is literally "neck-exposed," suggesting the laying back of an animal's head, thus exposing the neck to the knife.

There are lessons which we may learn from this discussion. Unconverted men and women, let God's word have its perfect work in your hearts. Remember that the day of revelation is coming. This world's acts will then stand out as stout witnesses against you. All that we have thought and felt will then be known to God and to the world. We are distinctly informed that by our words shall we be justified or condemned. No man could endure to have his neighbor know him for an hour as God has known him for his lifetime. Did men know themselves as God knows them they would be ready to condemn themselves as guilty in the light of their own conscience. We ought all to let God's word have its perfect work in us as fire to consume the dross, as a light to guide our steps, and as the voice of God summon us to duty.

Students of God's word, appreciate its worth as never before. It is clamoring for recognition in the colleges of the country. It is securing its place as the honored text-book in many of the most honored colleges. Shall men study Homer for his poetry, and refuse to study the inspired psalmist? Sophocles for his dramas, and refuse to study the mysterious and sublime Job? Shall men study Plato for his philosophy, and not the Apostle Paul? Shall men study Herodotus for his history, and pass over the matchless histories of this unique book? Believe in your deepest souls that the word of God is adapted to convict, to convert, and to sanctify the soul. Remember that at its bar the race shall be judged; remember that when all its critics are forgotten it will still remain as the sublimest and divinest book the world has ever known. The names of some of its fiercest critics in the past would never have been heard by the people of to-day, but for their association with its immortal life, and with that of its divine Lord.

Teachers and preachers, learn the importance of knowing how to use "the sword of the Spirit." You must know the qualities of this divine sword. It is the choicest sort of a blade. You must be quick of eye and supple of wrist. The sword needs a trained and courageous soldier to wield it. The soldier ought to know enough of anatomy to know the vulnerable parts of his foe. The surgeon must not cut at random; the farmer must not cast the seed on fallow ground if he expects a harvest. The physician must not prescribe medicine without making a careful diagnosis. So you must study the needs of men, you must believe their great need, their fearful hunger, and their lost condition; then you can apply God's word to supply their want, to feed their hunger, and to reveal Christ as the Saviour of their souls. God in heaven, make us wise in winning souls for Jesus Christ!

Many men have entered the arena to tilt against the Bible, and lately especially against the Pentateuch. Pharaoh strove against Moses, and he sank like lead into the Red Sea. Jannes and Jambres, the Egyptian magicians, "withstood Moses," and they are named only to show their defeat and humiliation. Lucian, Celsus, Porphyry, and Julian the Apostate, were the leaders of the opposition to Christ and his church in their respective generations. Porphyry was, without doubt, one of the most brilliant opponents which Christianity has ever had. He was a peerless heathen polemicist. He moved boldly into the arena; he was resolved to dethrone Jesus Christ. He anticipated many of the critical methods which are common in our day; but these men would be utterly forgotten were it not that they linked their names, even in opposition, with that Name which is above every name.

Jesus Christ is King. From his watch-tower in the heavens he rules this world. His pierced hand is on the helm of the universe. Men have, in their own opinion, been constantly engaged in overthrowing the Bible; but the work has to be constantly repeated. Never did any other book have such vitality. It constantly confronts its foes with new elements of power. It never was mightier than it is to-day. It has overthrown many forms of heathenism, and is now moving forward, with head erect and step triumphant, to the conquest of the world. Let us rejoice in its glorious characteristics, living, energetic, piercing, and discerning. God help us to use, obey, and love this immortal book!

IV

THE INSPIRED WITHOUTS

"That at that time ye were without Christ, being aliens from the commonwealth of Israel, and strangers from the covenants of promise, having no hope, and without God in the world." Eph. 2 : 12.

IV

THERE is a distinct gain, at times at least, in the method of pulpit treatment introduced by some popular evangelists, and known as Bible Readings. In this sermon the word "without" in several important connections will be discussed.

Take this first: "Without shedding of blood is no remission" (Heb. 9 : 22). In this passage we see that almost all things are by the law purified by blood. This is a truth that is taught constantly on the pages of both Testaments, and it is a truth which sets forth in its proper importance the atoning death of Jesus Christ. Some things, the apostle here teaches us and we are also taught elsewhere, are purified by fire, and still others by water. But the remission of sins was universally associated with the shedding of blood. No instance can be cited on the authority of Scripture of the forgiveness of human guilt except as the result of the shedding of blood. It would be impossible to name any one of God's relations to men more universal than this. If a man is to be saved his salvation must be secured in harmony with this divine law. If a man rejects that principle there is no other, so far as we know, on which he can base his hope of salvation. To set forth this truth was one of the great objects of the Old Testament dispensation, for it was a truth taught among Jews as truly as among Christians. And it is not difficult for us to discover the reason for this universal and divine law. Every sinner has virtually forfeited his life by his transgression against God, and because of his transgression the law of God requires his death. Life is the blood, and the blood of the victim is shed as a substitute for the life of the sinner. In harmony with this principle the victims offered in sacrifice typified the great sacrifice of Christ. He gave his life for the life of men, and because of his death all men, if they accept the offers of his mercy, may be saved.

This element in our holy religion has been made the subject of satirical comment and of fierce opposition. Many have violently opposed what they call "a bloody theology." We accept the sneering definition. It is quite correct; we glory in the atoning death of Jesus Christ, and we look forward to the time when we shall sing the song of the Lamb that was slain. If we have redemption, it is through his sacrifice; if we are justified, it is by his death; if we are washed, it is in this fountain of cleansing; if we have victory, it is through the blood of the Lamb; and if we are admitted to the white-robed throng in heaven, it will be because we have been cleansed in his blood.

Take again: "Without faith it is impossible to please him [God]" (Heb. 11 : 6). We now advance a step. If we have been admitted into the Christian life our great aim will be to please God, our Father and our Redeemer. We shall recognize this duty as our highest ambition and our most inspiring motive. But without an active faith, one which enables us to walk with God and to become like God, it is impossible that we can please him. In this chapter we have glorious tributes to the heroes and heroines of faith, and right in the midst of these historic examples of faith comes the general truth quoted at the head of this paragraph. We can readily understand that it is impossible to please God except as we manifest utter confidence in his promises, his wisdom, and his love. We certainly must believe that he is, before we can please him or render him any form of service, for if we deny his existence necessarily all relations to him at once cease. We must also, in order to have him rightly guide our lives, believe that he is a rewarder of those who diligently seek him.

The principle laid down here with reference to God is true in other relations of life as well as in religion. No child can please his parents except he repose faith in their word and manifest trust in their wisdom and affection. The basal principle of joy in married life is mutual confidence resulting in affection. Those whom we cannot trust we certainly cannot love. Trust precedes and presupposes all love worthy of the name. If a man will not believe the word of the living God, how can he please God? However much one may be disposed to doubt his fellowmen, let no one dare doubt the word of the Almighty. So doubting him we make him, as the Scripture has taught us, a liar. Surely men who take this position do not stop to realize the responsibility they assume, the infidelity they cherish, and the rebellion of which they are guilty. All the relations of business and friendship would be impossible but for the faith which men repose in each other. The whole world runs on the wheels of faith; destroy this faith and you practically annihilate the world. Every time a merchant sells a bill of goods or engages in almost any other business transaction he illustrates the power of faith. You cannot insult a man more than to express doubt as to his word. Is not the same thing true of God? And yet men constantly doubt his word, determinedly refuse to listen to his warnings, recklessly reject his tender invitations, and despise his sacred promises. If men would but believe God they would forsake their sins and become his dear children. Hearers or readers of these words who are not Christians, are guilty of the enormous crime of disbelieving the word of the Almighty. Few men realize the enormity, the blackness, the heinousness of this heaven-defying and soul-destroying sin. It is a matter of such seriousness that I cannot avoid presenting it to you in this solemn way. How long are you to continue to doubt and to oppose God? How long will you make the God of all holiness, truth, and love, a liar to his very face? I would scarcely use that expression were it not that the loving Apostle John sets me the example. Oh, believe now that God is; that he is from everlasting to everlasting; and believe also that he rewards those that seek him, and that by the laws of eternal justice he must punish those who refuse the offers of his love, who deny his word, and who thus destroy their own souls.

Once more: "Faith without works is dead" (James 2 : 26). Having entered upon the Christian life, and having placed before you as an object of attainment the desire to please God, we now see in the scripture just quoted the relation in which active service stands to the development of the Christian life. It is quite likely that when the Apostle James wrote these words there were those who taught that men were saved by a formal faith in the one true God. He therefore shows us that the only faith which avails for salvation is accompanied by good works. He shows that a dead faith is practically no faith, and that wherever there is genuine faith there will be good living as its result. He has said nothing more than the Apostle Paul has said in other forms in the second chapter of his Epistle to the Romans. The Apostle Paul often refutes the same Jewish error that is here opposed by James. Both practically assert that not the hearers, but the doers of the law shall be justified. Both show that a knowledge of God's law without a corresponding performance of the same only increases our condemnation. We are in the passage before us taught that there is as much necessity that faith and works be united to constitute true religion as that body and soul be united to form a real man. As the body without the spirit is dead, so we are taught that faith without Christian works is dead also. It is absolutely certain, both from the teachings of inspiration and from the nature of the case, that where there is true faith there will also be good works. If good works are wanting we are safe in affirming that faith is also wanting. James is not here, nor anywhere, arguing against genuine faith, but only against the supposition that mere formal and intellectual faith will save the soul. He shows that where there is the root of faith there will be the flower and fruit in good works. Except a man believe in Christ he cannot be saved, and except his faith reveal itself in good works we have no reason to believe that he has saving faith. We may affirm that no man can be saved by good works, and we are equally warranted in saying that no man can be saved without good works. I never could see why men are so troubled by the supposed difference on this subject between James and Paul. Many infidels, and especially Voltaire, have sneered at the imaginary contradiction between these two writers. At one time in his history Luther considered this difficulty to be insuperable, and so he was disposed to deny the inspiration of James. Later, however, he took a larger view of the subject and corrected his earlier teachings.

If we look at the matter fairly we shall see that there is no contradiction between these two writers. Each wrote from his own point of view. Paul looks at the entire subject of faith in relation to an unconverted man, but James speaks of faith in relation to a man who is converted, who has entered upon the Christian life, and who ought to manifest the fruits of the faith which saves. The Apostle Paul rightly teaches that a sinner is justified by faith, and the Apostle James rightly affirms that the faith which justifies is not a mere speculative belief, not a formal and dead faith, but one which brings forth fruit in the development of character and in the performance of good works. Paul rightly teaches that whatever gifts or graces a man may have, if he has not true faith in Christ he cannot receive forgiveness and justification; and James rightly teaches that whatever pretended faith a man may have, if he does not bring forth the fruits of the new life this faith is without value. There is, therefore, no contradiction whatever between these two writers. Each looks at the one subject from his own point of view; each could adopt the language of the other when his own view-point and ultimate purpose are admitted by the other. I can take my stand with the utmost earnestness beside Paul and say "amen" to every word he has written, and I can with equal earnestness and pleasure take my stand beside the Apostle James and say "amen" to every word that he has written.

The brilliant Frederick W. Robertson has, in his striking way, brought out the relation between faith and works as follows: "Suppose I say, 'A tree cannot be struck without thunder.' That is true; for there is never destructive lightning without thunder. But again, if I say, 'The tree was struck by lightning without thunder,' that is true too, if I mean that the lightning alone struck it without the thunder striking it. Yet the two assertions seem contradictory. So in the same way Paul says, faith justifies without works; that is, faith alone is that which justifies us, not works. There will be works with faith as there is thunder with lightning; but just as it is not the thunder but the lightning which strikes the tree, so it is not the works which justify. Put it then in one sentence, faith alone justifies, but not the faith which is alone. Lightning alone strikes, but not the lightning which is alone without thunder, for that is only summer lightning and harmless."

Still again: "Without chastisement" not true sons. (See Heb. 12 : 8.) We are now advancing in the Christian life. We have received remission through the shedding of blood, we possess the faith which pleases God and which manifests itself in the performance of good works, and we are now prepared to receive the chastisement which proves our sonship with God. Every true child of God must receive the training which corrects his faults, subdues his temper, rebukes his wanderings, and insures his obedience. The word chastisement here suggests wholesome discipline rather than severe punishment; it implies the training at home and the instruction at school of a well-disciplined child. God takes the tenderest relations of life to set forth his affection toward the children of men. In the one hundred and third Psalm and thirteenth verse we read: "Like as a father pitieth his children, so the Lord pitieth them that fear him"; and in the sixty-sixth chapter and thirteenth verse of Isaiah, "As one whom his mother comforteth, so will I comfort you." God may suffer unconverted men to remain in their sins without immediately inflicting chastisement; but he will not permit his dear children thus to remain in sin. Let us receive the chastisement which our Father sends with submissive hearts, with joyous spirits, and with obedient lives.

Take still another passage: "Holiness without which no man shall see the Lord" (Heb. 12: 14). Chastisement is conducive to holiness, and holiness proves our acceptance with God and assures us of an eternal residence in his presence. Many persons dislike the word holiness. It may be admitted that the word has often been used in such a manner as to justify to some degree the dislike. It has been associated with extravagant and one-sided views of divine truth and of Christian character. Nevertheless the word appears in Scripture in solemn exhortation, and no refinement of exegesis can remove it from the sacred page. It ought to be the constant endeavor of God's people to realize in their lives the character which this word suggests.

One element of holiness is wholeness in the service of God. Hale, health, whole, and holy, all stand in close linguistic relations. No man can be morally healthy except he be striving after holiness. It is certain that the Christian church needs men who have wholeness in God's service; far too many are half-hearted in the

Christian life. Whatever views we may hold regarding the higher life, technically understood, it is quite certain that all of us practically might live and ought to live a higher and holier life than most persons do. A great and solemn law is laid down in the passage at the head of this paragraph. By the words "see the Lord," we are to understand the enjoyment of his presence; and by the fundamental laws of our nature without likeness to his character we cannot enjoy his presence. There is a sense in which all men will see him, but not in the sense of dwelling with him in felicity. It is imposble that unforgiven and rebellious sinners could be introduced into heaven. Heaven is loving Christ and being like Christ. Men who do not love him cannot have any heaven anywhere; men who love him have heaven always and everywhere in proportion to the reality of that love. To take men to heaven who do not love him would be cruelty to them and to all heavenly beings. Many classes in our communities now are fit for prisons, but not fit to be members of respectable families. If all the guilty inhabitants of hell were brought into heaven at this moment, cherishing their present hatred of God, heaven would be no heaven to them. Heaven is a state, a condition, as truly as it is a place, and holiness is its distinctive characteristic. What would unholy men do in heaven? Of what could they speak? What songs could they sing? No untamed savage of the woods would be more out of place in a drawing room than an unconverted man in heaven. The frequenters of saloons and other abodes of sin would be absolutely wretched in a sweet and heavenly prayer meeting. The more heavenly the meeting the more wretched they would be. They would hastily leave it and return to the haunts of sin. Such men need new hearts, new wills, new loves. If a prayer meeting would give them misery, heaven would be really hell in their experience. Would that men could see that God is not arbitrary in his allotment of human souls! Would that men could see that there is a law of moral as truly as of physical gravitation, and that all men, in harmony with that universal and eternal law, must go to their own place! Holiness here will assuredly bring us to heaven hereafter. May we learn the solemn and blessed truth that without holiness no man shall see the Lord!

Look at another "without": "Without me ye can do nothing" (John 15 : 5). In the Christian life the blessed Christ is at its beginning, its middle, and its ending. We begin by gazing on him on the cross; we end by sitting with him on the throne. Most gracious is our Lord in this connection in acknowledging believing sinners to be branches of himself, the divine vine.

Only as we abide in this vine can we bear fruit. It is just as possible for the branch separated from the vine to live and bring forth fruit, as for us to do any good thing when separated from Christ. God can do without us, but we cannot live, move, and have our being, without God. It is not here said that without Christ we cannot do much, but it is affirmed that without him we can do nothing. A little time ago I assisted in trimming the vines in front of Calvary Church. We cut off a vine which appeared to be of little importance, but the next day we discovered that great sections of the leaves well up in front of the church were dying. We had separated them, with all their delicate tendrils, from vital connection with the living root, and their speedy decay was inevitable. O men and women who are depending on your own righteousness for salvation, hear these solemn words: "Without me ye can do nothing." You are hoping that in your own unaided strength you can bring forth the fruits of true discipleship, of noble character, and of divine sonship. You are terribly mistaken. As well might a man attempt to quench his thirst by drinking from the salty sea, as to satisfy his spiritual desires by the cup of self-righteousness. As well might a man lean on his own shadow for support as on his own righteousness for help and strength in performing duty and in developing character. O severed branches, you shall be withered, then gathered into bundles, then cast into the fire and burned. This is not my teaching, but Christ's. Without vital union with Christ you can accomplish really no good thing. O blessed branches, abide, I beseech you, in Christ. As every leaf in nature is in miniature in shape and veins the tree on which it grows, so every branch that abides in the heavenly vine shall bring forth leaves of conduct and character bearing close resemblance to the divine vine. So abiding in Christ we may claim the blessed promise, "Ye shall ask what ye will and it shall be done unto you."

Take now the text: "Without Christ . . . having no hope . . . without God." (Eph. 2 : 12). This verse contains a sad description of the former condition of those to whom the apostle wrote. Once they had not even heard of Christ; once they lived without the inspiration and consolation which the gospel of Christ brings. All Christians were once, to some degree at least, in a similar condition; they once lived as if Christ had never come into the world to save men; they once lived as if there were no heaven when this life is over. We are not surprised that the apostle adds, "having no hope." Some hope they and all men have, but the apostle means to say that they had no good hope, no well-grounded and enduring hope, for either time or eternity. Some men rest their hope on their self-righteous lives, but the day will come when this hope will be nothing more than "sinking sand." Some trust in the mere formalities of Christian service and in the intellectual adoption of Christian creeds; some trust in some vague way in the mercy of God as a ground for universal salvation. They forget that while God is abundant in goodness, in mercy, and in truth, he can bestow his mercy only in harmony with the conditions he himself has laid down.

The apostle proceeds to say that they were "without God in the world." This is the last characterization of these hopeless persons. This statement caps the climax of the hopeless condition of these Ephesians. It is true still of many men of the world; they live as if there were no God; as if there were no eternity; as if they themselves were only as the beasts that perish. They never worship God, they never read his word; they never recognize his existence. If it were authoritatively announced to-morrow that God is dead, they would make no change in their modes of thought or methods of living. Practically to them God is dead; they are as truly without God, as truly "*A-theoi*," as if God had never been. The announcement of his death would not affect them as much as the statement that the Czar of Russia or the

Sultan of Turkey were dead, or dethroned. It is unspeakably sad that men should so live. It is indescribably sorrowful that men made in the image of God should live without God; that travelers to eternity should pass over life's dusty highway as if there were no eternity.

I now beseech you, men and women, to repudiate this practical atheism, to give your hearts to the living God, and to consecrate your lives to his service. God help us to possess all the gifts and graces suggested by these inspired "Withouts," that we may be his true children here, and may dwell forever with him in heaven!

V

THE DEFENSIBLE HOPE

"But sanctify the Lord God in your hearts: and be ready always to give an answer to every man that asketh you a reason of the hope that is in you, with meekness and fear." 1 Peter 3 : 15.

V

WE are told that at the battle of Salamanca, Wellington commanded one of his officers to advance with his troops and to occupy a gap which the duke perceived in the lines of the French. The officer so commanded rode up to him and said, "My Lord, I will do the work, but first give me a grasp of that conquering right hand of yours." The grasp was given him and off he rode to the deadly attack. In our weakness a grip from Christ gives us indescribable strength. He is the fountain of all our life and power. The way to overcome human weakness is to receive divine strength. The best way, indeed the only way, to drive out darkness is to let in light; so the best way to avoid being terrified by the fear of men is to be sanctified by the fear of God. If we rightly fear God we shall never wrongly fear men. When the filial, fiducial, reverent fear of God is in the soul, weak and foolish fear of man can never control our thought and action. So we are commanded in the opening of this text to sanctify the Lord God in our hearts. The psalmist said, "What time I am afraid, I will trust in thee." The three faithful men in a critical experience in reference to Nebuchadnezzar's command, said, "We are not careful to answer thee in this matter. . . Our God whom we serve is able to deliver us from the burning fiery furnace, and he will deliver us out of thine hand, O king. But, if not, be it known unto thee, O king, that we will not serve thy gods, nor worship the golden image which thou hast set up." Sanctifying God in the heart is the true and only antidote against all fear of men in daily life. We sanctify the Lord Jesus when we truly love and serve him; we sanctify him when our lives before men are according to his will. But it is not my intention to enlarge upon the thought with which this text opens, important and beautiful though it is. That thought alone is worthy of an entire sermon. At this time I confine myself to the remaining clauses of the verse.

We are taught, in the first place, that every *Christian has a good reason for his hope.* A Christian's hope is always defensible. We repel with utmost scorn the idea that a man acts contrary to the highest reason when he submits to the lordship of Jesus Christ. The fact is that only as a man submits to this lordship does he act in harmony with the highest reason. The man who opposes Jesus Christ commits moral suicide. Faith is reason attaining its highest range and its loftiest reach. There are many things in religion above our reason; but they are not necessarily contrary to reason. They may be above my reason and yours; but is our reason the measure of the highest reason? If there is a God, and he has given us a book which is a revelation of himself, we must expect that book to contain many things far above the reason of men. There must be obscure and mysterious elements in any full revelation which the great God may make to finite men. Whenever and wherever the infinite comes into contact with the finite insoluble problems necessarily emerge. This result is due to the limitations of human attainments and possibilities. Many difficulties of thought and belief were experienced before Christianity was introduced, and are equally experienced now among thoughtful men where Christianity is unknown. These difficulties are due to our finite conditions and to our human limitations. The great thoughts of the Almighty cannot be crowded into our finite understanding. The spirituality of religious things makes it impossible for men, so largely under the influence of sensuous thoughts and material conditions, fully to understand lofty truths. Many of these truths are not reducible to human formulæ; they are vastly above our complete comprehension. We can apprehend God, but we cannot fully comprehend God. These great truths can be understood only as they enter into our natures and control our lives as a result of our personal experience of their reality. There are heavenly bodies with whose movements we are not entirely familiar. So far as our knowledge of the solar system is concerned, the movements of these bodies are above and beyond reason. Our laws do not fully explain their vast orbits, but there are doubtless laws of the heavenly bodies not yet fully discovered. The movements described are not contrary to a higher law, although beyond all the laws with which we are familiar.

Possibly none of the miracles of Christ were contrary to nature. In a certain sense they were *super*-natural; but they never were and never ought to be represented as *contra*-natural. They were contrary to the laws with which we ordinarily are familiar; but they were in entire harmony with higher laws, some of which are beyond the range of our present knowledge. When Christ turned the water into wine he simply accelerated processes which are constantly going forward. The same remark applies to the increase of the loaves, and to many other of his miracles. He often found many things in an abnormal state through the presence and power of sin; he simply by the exercise of divine power restored them to their normal condition. By the interposition of a higher law he held the lower law in check for the time being. The higher law of preservation in salt holds in control the lower law of decay in meat. I hold this book in my hand, and thus check the natural workings of the law of gravitation which would bring the book suddenly down to my pulpit. There is no contradiction in this action of the law of gravitation; there is simply the introduction, for the time being, of a higher law which holds the lower law in leash.

God nowhere is a violator of law. In the vast range of his universe he honors the laws which he himself has made. He constantly appeals to our reason in justification of his own claims upon us. Through his servant Isaiah, God commands us to reason together with himself; and through the Apostle Paul he exhorts us to prove all things. Christianity asks no favors; it simply demands justice. No man ought to entertain opinions for which a good reason cannot be given. He may not be able to give the reason in all its fullness, but his inability so to do ought not to be taken as equivalent to the holding of reasonless beliefs.

There are three kinds of evidence for the truth of Christianity, and each is unanswerable within its own sphere; they are historical, internal, and experimental. The strongest, however, in our practical work is the experimental. The derivation of the word shows that it refers to truths which come out of us, or are held by us, because they have gone through us. We all understand that no man can testify to the power of certain remedies in medicine as can the man who has been thereby entirely cured of dangerous diseases. A man must be inside the circle of Christian influence in order to testify to its power. No man can appreciate the glory of a painted window, as seen by the sunlight, except he be within the cathedral into which the light comes through the pictured glass. The Christian faith is a splendid cathedral, and light from the face of God streams through its divinely pictured windows. He who stands without in daytime sees no splendor nor glory. Only he who is within discovers the matchless beauty and indescribable splendor of the heavenly light streaming through the glorious windows. So only he who does the will of God, as our Lord has taught us, can know whether the doctrine is of God. It is useless for men to discuss historic questions and oppose conclusions on supposed historic grounds, if intelligent experience contradicts these imaginary conclusions. Mr. Beecher illustrated this thought by representing a number of historical students deliberating as to whether or not a certain harp was David's harp. One opposes this view, because the wood bears evidence of never having come down from olden times. He is sure that it is modern wood. Another is absolutely certain that the strings are of recent date. Still another is sure that it cannot be David's harp of solemn and harmonic sound because this one is so unmusical as not to deserve the name of a harp; but while they are discussing the matter a " gray-bearded old harper comes in, and instead of answering their objections takes a stool, and sits up to the harp, and sweeping his hand from side to side over the strings, wakes its long-forgotten sounds, and rings out the ballad or the hymn; and then these men sit entranced. They labored to prove that the instrument was not capable of giving forth music; but they neglected to try it. And the moment the old harper laid his hands on it, it was its own argument, and it put to silence its defamers."

The argument from experience is that of the blind man who was healed by Christ. He could not meet the cavils of the captious Pharisees, but all the Pharisees in Jerusalem could not take from him the glorious experience that though he once was blind he now saw. The argument of many opposers of religion is absolutely worthless, because they have never had true religion. They are speaking of what, in the deepest sense, they know nothing. All the blind men in America could not make me believe that the sun is not bright, nor that the rainbow is not beautiful. They are not competent witnesses. Experimental knowledge comes home with tremendous power. Only those who know it can appreciate its force. Only he who has tasted food can testify to its power of nourishment. The maniac who cut himself with stones and wandered in the tombs, but is now sitting, clothed and in his right mind at the feet of Jesus, is an unanswerable argument to the power of Jesus. Many who hear or may read these words can testify to the value of experimental knowledge of Christ and his salvation. Your faith in God has supported you in the heaviest trials; it has soothed your keenest sorrows; it has allayed your fears, and it has brightened your hopes. The evidence of a pure life is an irresistible argument for the truth of Christianity. In the year 1848 Lamartine introduced De la Eure to the riotous populace, saying: "Listen, citizens, it is a pure life of sixty years that is about to address you." That was a marvelous introduction. Sixty years of a pure life behind sermons or orations make them mighty arguments and give them resistless power. God give us this experimental knowledge of his Son Jesus Christ!

We remark, in the second place, that every Christian ought to be *ready to give the reason for his hope*. He ought always to be able to give it, and also, on all suitable occasions, to be willing to give this reason. Our position as members of the church of Christ challenges inquiry. Men have the right to ask us questions regarding our our faith. In our baptism, by the very act, we separated ourselves from the world. We sit to-day at this table of the Lord while others retire;

and we ought to ask ourselves the reason for the difference between us and them; and they, doubtless, will ask such questions. We ought not to regard questions of this sort, when asked at the right time and in the proper spirit, as impertinent intrusions; rather ought we to regard them as furnishing an opportunity for doing good to men and for giving honor to Christ. Doubtless there are times when giving an answer might be somewhat like casting pearls before swine; doubtless there are times when silence is golden. In matters of this sort, as in all other matters, we must exercise sanctified common sense. There is a time to speak and there is a time to be silent; there are times when speech is only silvern, and then silence is golden.

The word apology, or defense, the literal translation of the original word rendered in our version "answer," does not mean an excuse for our faith as if it were wrong. The word originally was used as a defense of what was right and true. In our ordinary use of the word "apology," which comes from the original word here employed, we give it a changed meaning, making it equivalent to an excuse. This fact led Robert Hall to say, "Bishop Watson's 'Apology for the Bible' is a good book with a bad title." A defense of our religious faith might include all three of the kinds of evidence of which I have spoken. Probably it was the experimental evidence which the inspired writer of the text had especially in mind. Christians in our day must so advance in knowledge as to be able to defend the truth from attack. It is still true that the experimental evidence is the most powerful. This evidence, as suggested, the Apostle Paul constantly introduced. He related his experience of the power of God's truth upon his own soul.

Perhaps the church of to-day is in danger of neglecting this element of power. A statement of Christian experience was one of the greatest elements of power in the early days of Methodism; and scarcely less so among Baptists. Let us be sure that we have a well-founded hope of heaven; that we are resting on the rock Christ Jesus, and then let our answer be always ready in defense of our faith. While we ought not to be obtrusive and indiscreet, we ought still to be always willing when the fitting time comes to speak the fitting word. If heaven's joys are in our souls they will often be on our tongues. If we live with Jesus, men will take knowledge of that fact. If the love of Christ be in our hearts it cannot long be hid. If the rose of Sharon be in our bosom, it will fill the atmosphere in which we move with its fragrance. If we are Christ's, men will know the fact by the tones of our voice, the grasp of our hand, the glance of our eye, and the dominant spirit of our entire lives.

Tell out this blessed experience. Tell it to every one, rich and poor, learned or ignorant; tell it to all of every nation and in every land. Tell how once you were without God and without hope; tell of Christ's wondrous love; and tell of your joy in believing in him.

Every Christian, in the third place, ought to *give his answer in a becoming spirit*—"with meekness and fear." Much depends upon the spirit in which our answer is given. We may speak right words in a wrong way. We may tear down by our manner what we wish to build up by our matter. The manner is often more than the matter. Many a warm-hearted, earnest, loving Christian has done more to convince an opponent than the most learned, but harsh defender of Christianity could do. A loving heart makes an eloquent tongue. A Christian ought to lift up his head in any presence. He is a son of God, an heir of glory, and a joint-heir with Jesus Christ. He is the highest style of man. True meekness is the climax of manliness. Christianity introduced a higher type of manliness than was ever before known. Often in classic Greek, words indicative of humility were allied to meanness. Christianity introduced new thoughts into the languages of the world. Some of these thoughts required new words for their proper expression; they sometimes burst the old words with their fullness of meaning. Virtue to the ancient Roman meant simply physical bravery; it lacked the noble moral quality now associated with the word. Christianity gave to the word meekness its exalted meaning and its sweet and gentle spirit. The modesty which religion inculcates is always an element of power. The man who cannot control himself cannot control his fellow-men. Temperance, as used in Scripture, means self-control over the entire life. The man who loses his temper has lost power over men because he cannot exercise control over himself.

It is implied in the text that Christians would sometimes be unkindly assailed, and that questions would often be asked in a taunting and insulting manner. Still they were to keep their temper; they were not to give way to feelings of resentment or revenge. Christian meekness is true manliness. It stands for that which is kingliest in man, queenliest in woman, and Christliest in both. The Bible speaks of but three men whose faces shone with holy light, Christ, Moses, and Stephen; and they were men whose meekness was as marked as their faces were bright. Sir Walter Raleigh was once spat upon in public by a hot-headed youth who challenged him to mortal combat. Taking out his handkerchief the noble knight made this reply: "Young man, if I could as easily wipe your blood from my conscience as I can this injury from my face, I would this moment take your life." It is said that the misguided youth was so struck with his own misconduct and with Sir Walter's nobility that he fell upon his knees and sought forgiveness.

The meekness here endorsed is accompanied by fear—the fear which grows out of a reverent spirit, not the fear of those who propose a question regarding the reasons for religious faith and life. True fear drives out false fear. Let us have clear and definite views of Christian truth, and then let us deem it a high privilege to be witnesses for God. Bravely, joyously let us confess Christ before men. "The fear of man bringeth a snare." Spurn that fear as unworthy of a child of God. Shame came into the world because of sin, and shame ought never to be experienced except in connection with sin. Stand up in the presence of men and demons and boldly give a reason for the hope that is within you. Let us be ashamed of cowardice and sin, but never of our faith, and certainly never of our Lord.

We are then clearly to understand that all true Christian believers ought to have a good reason for their faith in Christianity as true. We ought all to strive to be familiar with the evidences of the truth of our holy faith; this faith is founded on evidence which may be fully understood and clearly stated. It is not, indeed, to be expected that every believer will understand all forms of Christian evidences, nor that each disciple can meet all the objections to revealed religion which its enemies may present. But all mature Christians can give sufficient evidence to justify their faith and to meet the arguments of opposers. We ought to welcome the opportunity of testifying to all men regarding our religious hope. Too seldom do we converse about our religious faith. Too often do we give objectors reason to suppose that our religious convictions are simply the result of education, or perhaps merely of tradition.

The humblest believer may have experimental arguments which no amount of skepticism can resist. The devout and consistent Christian, however unlettered he may be, may so live his religion that no amount of argument can resist the power of his godly example; he may so live that all men will take knowledge of him that he has been with Jesus. A consistent life is unanswerable testimony in favor of religion. When the testimony of lip and life is harmonious, no weapon hurled against us can harm our character or our religion. Let us then ring out our loyalty to our Lord and our unswerving devotion to his truth, being ready always and everywhere to give a defense for the sure and certain hope which we have in our most holy faith.

VI

THE CHRISTIAN GRACES

"But the fruit of the Spirit is love, joy, peace, longsuffering, gentleness, goodness, faith, meekness, temperance: against such there is no law." Gal. 5 : 22, 23.

VI

IN the preceding verses we have an account of what are called the works of the flesh. It is evermore true that what is born of the flesh is flesh, and what is born of the Spirit is spirit. But in the text we pass from darkness to light; from sin to holiness; from the region of sorrow and death to that of life, light, and joy. The fruit of the Spirit, as here described, is a glorious list of Christian graces. It is always true that the right spirit among men is born of the presence and power of the Holy Spirit of God. The divine Spirit is the sacred fountain whence flow blessed and divine streams in human character and influence. We often speak of the "fruits" of the Spirit; but it is interesting to observe here that the apostle does not say "fruits" but "fruit." He seems carefully to avoid the plural and to choose the singular form of the word. Strictly speaking, there is only one fruit of the Spirit; but that one fruit manifests itself in many blessed forms.

It will be profitable for us to examine these Christian graces, this holy fruit, in the order given us in the text. Our attention is first called to *Love* as an element in the fruit of the

Spirit. Rightly does the noble apostle begin with love. Love is the foundation stone in this sublime and divine structure. Love is the first link in this golden chain; love is the brightest jewel in this royal crown. Love is an abridgement of the divine law, and is a fundamental precept in the holy gospel. Finely does Luther call it "the shortest and longest divinity; shortest for the form of words; long, yea everlasting, for the use and practice, for love never shall cease." Love is the true spirit prompting right action in every line of Christian duty. Love covers a multitude of sins. Love is the feet of duty running out in the path of obedience; love is the hands of duty dispensing blessings. Love is never puffed up; but is kind in heart, lowly in spirit, and helpful in service. The love mentioned in the text includes love both to God and man; but perhaps love to men is intended to be especially prominent. The apostle is here placing the fruit of the Spirit in opposition to the thoughts and acts which spring from an unregenerate, and so unloving, heart. Love is therefore the bond of perfectness, and the true touchstone of all creeds and Confessions. It is the heart and soul of all true religion. Well did Mr. Beecher, quoting the words, " Now abideth faith, hope, love—these three, but the greatest of these is love,' add, " For love is the seraph, and faith and hope are but the wings by which it flies." Love, we are clearly taught in the thirteenth chapter of First Corinthians, excels eloquence, excels knowledge, excels faith and hope, excels all other gifts. Going back to the figure underlying the text, we may say that love is the juice of the fruit, and the juice is sweet both to God and to men. May God give us this blessed fruit of the divine Spirit, "Love divine, all love excelling."

The next element in the fruit of the Spirit is *Joy*. The joy here meant springs from a realization of the love of God in the soul; it is joy in the evidence of forgiveness; it is the holy exultation which springs from a sense of pardon. It is joy arising from the performance of duty, from the endurance of trial, and from the hope of heaven. There is matchless and marvelous joy in suffering and in laboring for Christ. There is joy in the new discoveries the Christian makes of the love of God, and the blessings which that love constantly imparts. He has never truly known joy who has not experienced the blessedness of working for God in the conversion of souls and in the comforting of saints. Compared with this, all other joy is sorrow, all other brightness is darkness; all other peace is turmoil, all other bliss is misery. Unconverted men have a joy which is comparable to the joy of the Christian only as lightning is comparable to light; lightning scorches and blasts, but light is helpful and healing. The joy of a sinner is as the crackling of thorns under a pot; it is a joy that is temporary; it is a joy that leaves behind it the stings of conscience and the goads of memory. But the Christian's joy is peaceful, beautiful, exultant, radiant, eternal. It is a joy resulting from the consciousness of God's presence, from harmony with God's will, and from the assurance of walking in the path of holy obedience. It is a joy which is a balm in the miseries of life, and which is a foretaste of the blessedness of heaven. Never was there a greater mistake than is made by those who represent the Christian life as one of darkness and gloom. A life without joy is a life without power; it is a life like an instrument out of tune. Joy in the Christian life is not simply a privilege; it is a duty. We are positively commanded to rejoice. The Apostle Paul distinctly says, "Rejoice in the Lord always: and again I say, Rejoice."

Only a Christian really has a right to rejoice. Unconverted men and women might well march through this world with bowed heads, with aching hearts, and keeping step to funeral music; but the Christian has even here a foretaste of the joy of the angels of heaven. He hears even now strains of heavenly music, and feels the uplift of the divine presence. Men of the world are dependent upon external circumstances for joy; their joy is merely happiness; it is merely what "haps" or falls to them from without. But the Christian's delight is not merely happiness, but joy; it is that which springs up from within and is, to a great degree, independent of external conditions. Blessed are they who rejoice constantly in the Lord their God; they, and only they, know real joy, a joy which the world can neither give nor take away.

The next fruit of the Spirit, as given in this blessed category, is *Peace*. This peace is the result of reconciliation with God. It is peace within the conscience of the believer; and it is peace which is deep and which cannot be disturbed by the varied experiences of life. It is peace which Christ sheds abroad in the heart; a peace which expels all disturbing conditions, and which is in the soul as the music of heaven, without a jarring strain or a discordant note. There is a calm in the soul like that which is in the ocean far below the stormy surface. We know that these surface waters may flow in fury before the hurricane; they may dash themselves in huge waves and wild foam, but beneath these surface waters, there are mighty depths where winds never blow, and waves never roll, depths calm as an autumn noon, depths peaceful as a summer evening, when not even a zephyr disturbs the unbroken calmness. Amid the varying noises of the world the believer enjoys this peace; amid its cares he has repose; amid its disappointments he has sweet realizations; amid its surface storms he has an inner calm, a calm which is like the unruffled peace of God himself. Unconverted men strive to call their anxieties nothing, and try to quiet them by chanting some siren song, saying to their souls, "Peace, peace, when there is no peace." For "there is no peace, saith the Lord, unto the wicked."

Nothing is more certain than this solemn statement. Wicked men cannot know substantial peace in the business or the pleasures of life; they can have no peace of conscience in their moments of moral thoughtfulness. They certainly cannot have a substantial peace on a bed of death; they can have no peace at the judgment bar of God; they can have no peace when banished from the presence of God. But blessed are God's true children, concerning whom we read "great shall be the peace of thy children." Jesus Christ came into the world as "the Prince of Peace." The angels sang the song of "peace on earth" the night he was born. The entire tendency of his reign was to promote universal peace. Before he left his disciples on the night on which he was betrayed, he said: "These things I have spoken unto you that ye might have peace"; and he also said to them, "Peace I leave with you, my peace I give unto you." He desired to impart to them the peace which he himself enjoys, that peace, which the apostle tells us "passeth all understanding." His first salutation to his disciples, on the evening of his resurrection day when he stood in the midst of them, was, "Peace be unto you." God is spoken of repeatedly by the Apostle Paul "as the God of peace." Thrice blessed are those in whose souls peace abides. This peace is the soul's celestial music; it is the first experience of that peace which is part of the believer's blessedness in eternity.

Another element in the Spirit's fruit is *long-suffering*. The word here used strictly means long-mindedness. It is the patient bearing of the reproaches received for Christ's sake; it is also a manifestation of patience with the frailties of others. It is the spirit which leads us to forgive the wrong done by others, because God, for Christ's sake has forgiven us. We know that the mind makes the man; tools do not really make the workman. Many of the noblest discoveries were made with very imperfect apparatus. Benjamin West made his first brushes out of a cat's tail; and Rittenhouse, who became the distinguished astronomer, first calculated eclipses on his plow handle. An internal condition resulting from great-mindedness makes us, in our endurance of criticism, largely independent of the critics. Large-mindedness is one of the noblest traits of man, as it is one of the best gifts of God. There is a greatness of soul which makes us heroes, whatever our external circumstances may be. He who can bear false charges, upheld by the consciousness of noble motives and exalted aims, is superior to the bitterness of such charges. He is a king among men; he can be calm as a June morning, however much others storm about him and at him. He is like a rock against which the waves beat; he is like a lighthouse while his critics are the flies which dash into and are consumed by the steady flame. The Apostle Paul well knew what it was to possess and manifest the grace of long-suffering. He would rather suffer wrong than do wrong; he would rather hope all things and believe all things, than be guilty of uncharitableness of thought or unkindness of action. Let us study to be so filled with the Spirit of Christ that we shall not be disturbed by the opposition of men, or even the onsets of Satan. He who fears God fully, need fear none besides.

Another grace is *Gentleness*. The word here so translated is also translated kindness. It means goodness, kindness, benignity; it is opposed to all harshness of temper, and all crabbedness of disposition. It includes mildness, calmness, and urbanity of disposition. This grace is one of the natural effects of the Spirit's presence in the soul. True religion never sours, but always sweetens, the temper; never makes the nature irritable, but always gentle and gracious. True religion is sunshine, joy, and peace; true religion is the school of true politeness. The Golden Rule, as given by our Lord, is the fundamental law of true etiquette. Politeness can be learned in the school of Christ better than in that of any Chesterfield. Courtesy is an important element in Christianity. Archdeacon Hare has said that a Christian is God Almighty's gentleman; and we may add that in a very real sense, Christ was the first gentleman of the world. The spirit of Christ in the heart makes men considerate of their fellow-men, and such consideration is a distinguishing element of gentlemanly deportment. Piety and politeness are closely related; rudeness and boorishness are far removed from true religious experience and conduct. There is no religious virtue in social ugliness. The spirit dwelling in the soul produces gentleness in the life. Gentleness carpets the rough path in life, puts a pillow under the aching head, and furnishes a sweet solace for the weary heart. The gentleness of Jesus gave him irresistible power; and every Christian ought to be able, humbly and joyously, to say concerning God, as the psalmist has taught us, "Thy gentleness hath made me great."

Another fruit of the Spirit is *goodness*. This word is doubtless here used in the sense of doing good, in the sense of beneficence. There is a marked difference between beneficence and benevolence. Benevolence is simply good in thought, in purpose, in feeling, in volition; but beneficence is good in action, in doing, in achieving. In this passage we are not simply taught to abstain from evil, but actually to perform good. We have not, therefore, a negative, but a positive quality, endorsed and emphasized. We are to follow the example of our blessed Lord, who went about doing good. Goodness, as here presented, is a progressive determination, not only to be good, but to do good. It is love actually at work for God and for man. It is love, as has been said, "with its hand at the plow; love with a burden on its back." It is love feeding the hungry, clothing the naked, watching beside the sick, guiding the blind, teaching the ignorant, and helping all men in every possible way. It is love, also, going with the message of the gospel to the heathen; it is love going with Howard to the wretched prisons of the world, and with Carey and Judson carrying the precious light of life to those dying in ignorance and sin. Goodness is greatness; he who is truly a good man is really a great man. Greatness of this character is within the reach of all men.

Still another grace of the Spirit is *faith*. Probably the word is used here in the sense of fidelity; it denotes a faithful man in his relations to his fellow-men, rather than a man of faith, in the technical sense, in his religious relations to God. The apostle's purpose here is not so much to illustrate the feeling one may have toward God, as it is to emphasize the influence of the Spirit over our lives in our relations with those about us. True religion makes men faithful in all their relations with their fellow-men. It makes a man faithful as a pastor to his people; a man faithful as a lawyer to his client; faithful as a physician to his patient; faithful as an employer to his employees, and also as an employee to the employer. It makes men faithful as husbands, fathers, and sons, as friends and as neighbors; faithful in all their contracts, promises, and endeavors. All professions of religion, not accompanied by faithful performances, are valueless. Consistent Christian lives are irresistible arguments for the divinity of Christianity. The best argument for Christianity is Christianity. If we are not loving to men whom we see, how can we show that we are loyal to God, whom we do not see?

The next grace enumerated here is *meekness*. This is one of the noblest of all qualities of the Christian life. It includes patience toward the erring, it implies the suffering of an injury without the desire for revenge. It is, in many respects, the balancing of all the other qualities of the soul. It is far removed from meanness; Christianity has given dignity and glory to the milder virtues in character; it has made lowliness, loftiness, and meekness, mightiness. Virtue to the ancient Roman meant simply physical bravery; the noble moral quality which we now attach to the word, was entirely wanting in Greek and Roman thought. Christianity puts a new and higher meaning into these old words; it makes virtue now the synonym of moral goodness, of rectitude, and of all that opposes vice. In like manner meekness has been exalted to its true and to its noble place in the dictionaries of the world, and in the thought, experience, and practice of noble souls whose lives are governed by him who said, "I am meek and lowly in heart." The promise of Christ is that the meek shall inherit the earth. In a real sense, the truly meek man inherits the earth here and now. He lives in a condition of enviable peace, and in the exercise of genuine power. Meekness is inseparable from true greatness; it adds beauty to the character and lustre even to the countenance. Attention has been called to the fact that we read only of three in Scripture whose faces shone—Christ, Moses, and Stephen; and we know that they were all conspicuous examples of meekness. Meekness in its true sense is learned in the school of Christ. When we empty ourselves of self, and are filled with the

Spirit of God; when we put off the robe of self-righteousness, and put on the Lord Jesus Christ, then we are meek in the right sense of that great word.

The last virtue mentioned in this remarkable catalogue is *temperance*. The word in the original has a much broader meaning, however, than our word temperance. It means, as its composition clearly shows, self-control. It indicates that we are to obtain the mastery over all our purposes, passions, and propensities. We have come to limit our word, for the most part, to abstinence from intoxicating liquors; but that meaning is only one element which enters into this great and strong word. It includes the dominion over every evil desire, and every unholy purpose. This is the word used by the Apostle Paul in his great address to Felix, when as the apostle "reasoned of righteousness, temperance, and judgment to come, Felix trembled." Here he teaches Felix the duty of control of all passions and inclinations. It is a lesson of prudence, chastity, and moderation in the largest sense of these words. The use of the word in this connection was eminently appropriate because of the relations maintained between Felix and Drusilla. Paul wished to bring him to repentance and so used this form of exhortation. In the passage immediately before us we are taught that the influences of the Holy Spirit upon the heart of Christians will make them moderate in all lawful indulgences; will early restrain them from sinful propensities, and from wicked pursuits. The word may indeed be applied to restraint from excessive indulgence in intoxicating drinks; but it covers the whole range of thought and feeling regarding all that is inherently evil, and all that may become evil by undue indulgence. A Christian man must be master of himself; no man can fully rule others except he first rule himself. No man can rightly command but the one who has learned wisely to obey. We master law by submitting to law; opposing any right law we are destroyed by law.

All who manifest the graces of character given in this catalogue are free from law, because they are in harmony with this highest law. The apostle follows the catalogue of virtues with the statement, "against such there is no law." There is no law to condemn such persons; the servant of God is the true freeman; all others are slaves. The servant of God rises above all other service; he who fears God truly, fears none other, even partially. A life of sin is a life of slavery. God help us all to know the glorious liberty of the children of God! God help us all to adorn the crown of our Christian character by these resplendent jewels—love, joy, peace, longsuffering, gentleness, goodness, faith, meekness, and temperance!

VII

THE DESIRABLE GROWTH

"But grow in grace and in the knowledge of our Lord and Saviour Jesus Christ." 2 Peter 3 : 18.

VII

FROM the discussion in the chapter from which the text is taken, it is certain that the apostle feared that there was danger lest believers should be drawn away from the simplicity of their faith and from the constancy of their obedience. In order that they might be fortified against these dangers he earnestly exhorts them to grow in grace and in the knowledge of our Lord and Saviour Jesus Christ. This thought occupies a prominent place in the apostle's teaching. He deemed it of so much importance that he gives it great prominence in the closing words of this last Epistle. If anything were needed to give emphasis to these words, the place which they here occupy would secure for them the needed attention and the necessary emphasis. No truth is more frequently taught in the word of God than that the life of a Christian is to be a continuous growth. As born of God he is a little child; he then passes on to the period of youth, and finally reaches the condition of full stature in the Lord. On the subject of growth we need line upon line, precept upon precept, here a little and there a great deal. It thus becomes necessary constantly to repeat this closing exhortation of this Epistle of the Apostle Peter. Religion is here spoken of as consisting in grace and knowledge. It is not uncommon to represent religion by a single word or by several words. Sometimes it is represented by faith, sometimes by love, sometimes by hope, sometimes by peace, or by some other equally significant word. It is here represented as consisting in growth in Christian grace and knowledge. To know Christ aright is to know the very heart of Christian truth, and to make progress in Christian experience. The ripest Christian knows yet but little of the Lord Jesus Christ. The more we know the more we feel our ignorance, and the greater is our desire for fuller knowledge. Even the Apostle Paul needed to know God more fully, for much as he knew he realized that there was vastly more yet to be learned.

No angel in heaven has yet exhausted the knowledge which God can impart, and the glories which his character suggests and illustrates. Right views of his person, his character, and his work, are the sum and essence, the heart and crown, of the Christian religion. The man who has a complete knowledge of Jesus Christ possesses all that is really essential to his welfare in time, and to his blessedness in eternity. Whatever a man may know of the learning of earthly schools, if he is ignorant of Jesus Christ he is ignorant indeed. Though he may be profoundly skilled in all science, if he knows not the science of salvation he is pitifully blind and ignorant. He may know all other characters of history, but if he knows not Jesus Christ he has never known true excellence in character, greatness in intellect, purity in heart, and divinity in humanity. The school of Christ is the noblest of all universities. The man who sits in the lowliest place at Jesus' feet is the man best prepared steadily to walk on the dizziest heights of human learning. Only the graduate of Christ's school on earth can be a matriculate in the celestial university where saints and seraphs may be his fellow-students. The man who knows not the grace and knowledge of Jesus Christ is without the knowledge which pertains to his highest development on earth and to his full blessedness in eternity.

But even if we have come to know Christ as our personal Saviour, and have some adequate conception of the knowledge which he imparts, growth is still our privilege and duty. When we are exhorted to grow in grace, the exhortation is equivalent to a command to increase in all that constitutes true religion and in the perfect development of Christian character. The entire Bible is full of exhortations similar in purport. The presence of inward spiritual life implies and secures growth in outward Christian acts. Dead trees do not grow; living trees must grow or soon cease to be living trees. If in this glorious springtime there are plants and trees which give no evidence of growth, we are warranted in affirming that they are not possessed of life. In the vast laboratory of God, marvelous forces making for growth are now at work in blade and plant and tree. Soon the living trees in our parks will be beautiful in the blossoms of spring and in the verdant garments of summer. But if amid this wonderful array of living forces there are trees which show no signs of life, we are warranted in affirming that they are dead. Leaf, blossom, and flower are the certain outcome of life in root and branch. When trees thus reveal their inner life, can we not predicate the existence of that life?

In the parable of the sower we learn that the seed is sown, and that it springs up in various places, but in many cases, dies away. Only in one case is there true life, and this life is shown by the fruit which the plant bears. The godly man is compared to a tree that "bringeth forth its fruit in its season." He is also likened to the tree that "spreadeth out her roots by the river, neither shall cease from yielding fruit." It is also affirmed that he shall flourish like the palm tree, that he shall grow as a cedar in Lebanon, that he shall be as the lily and grow as the vine. If we do not find Christians growing in this way, we are sure that they possess but a weak and sickly life, if they have life at all. Those who do not grow in grace soon die. No man can live upon past grace. No political party can live upon its past achievements, however patriotic and renowned. No religious denomination can long live upon its dead heroes and saints, however illustrious they may have been in their lives and however glorious in their attainments. Political parties, religious denominations, and individual Christians must bring forth fruit now, must recognize present obligations, and must achieve present victories. Failing in these respects, they will live a sickly life or die a speedy death. As well might a man expect to support his body on yesterday's food as to nourish his soul on yesterday's grace. No man ought to look back at the time of his conversion for the proofs of that conversion. A growing Christian finds the evidence of his Christianity in his present attainments, and in his brightening aspirations. The man who is obliged to look back through several years to the time of his conversion for the proof of its reality has reason to fear that he never was converted.

The figure of a race, which is so often found in the word of God, teaches the duty, the possibility, and the method of progress. The Apostle Paul teaches us not to rest satisfied with present attainments. He had run long and well, still he says, "Not as though I had already attained, neither were already perfect." He pressed forward constantly toward the mark of the prize. He daily forgot the things that were behind, forgot his triumphs, forgot his failures, and reached forth unto the things that were before. His was constantly an upward calling; high to-day, it was to be higher to-morrow, and still higher the day after. We are elsewhere taught that the path of the just is a light that shineth more and more unto the perfect day.

Growth in religion is as natural as in any other faculty of the soul. Often its beginnings are very feeble; our Lord anticipated this truth and gave encouragement in such a case. He likens faith to a grain of mustard seed, which is the smallest of all seeds. But if the faith is genuine, it will grow as did the mustard seed, which finally became a tree with birds lodging in its branches. At the first, faith may be like a blade of grass, then the ear, and after that the full corn in the ear. Religion is as susceptible of growth as any other faculty of the mind or virtue of the heart. All professors of religion who have become eminent for piety developed their religious faculties as the result of a definite purpose and by the use of appropriate means. No Christian ever becomes distinguished for faith, zeal, and consecration as the result of accident. As well might a man expect to become eminent for learning without earnest study, as to expect to grow in divine grace and knowledge without putting forth the necessary effort and using the divinely appointed means. Men have no more religion than they determine to have. If they want but little they will have but little. If they are willing to pay the price in self-abnegation and self-consecration, in giving up all they have and are to the service of God and man, they shall have piety in the most eminent degree. No men become Bunyans and Baxters, Wesleys and Whitefields, Spurgeons and Moodys, except as they give themselves up body and soul to the service of God. "Men may rise on stepping-stones of their dead selves to higher things"; but we must die to self if we are thus to rise and are truly to live to God. Half-hearted Christians know nothing of the living power, the actual joy, and possible bliss of Christians who lay themselves as living sacrifices on the altar of Jesus Christ. Let us remember that the Christian life is governed by laws as universal and uniform as gravitation and as eternal as God. If Christians conform their lives to these irresistible laws they will grow in stature; but if they do not, they will become pitiful dwarfs in the Christian life. No more painful is the physical dwarf in the midst of laughing, romping, growing, and joyous children than is the stunted Christian among stalwart men and beautiful women in the church and army of the Lord. A Christian ought never to sing, and a growing Christian never will sing:

> Where is the blessedness I knew
> When first I saw the Lord?
> Where is the soul-refreshing view
> Of Jesus and his word?

Parts of the hymn from which these lines are taken are exquisitely beautiful and entirely appropriate as the prayer of a growing Christian; but the plaintive cry uttered in these words will never be heard from the lips of a believer who is advancing in divine grace and knowledge. It is quite true that often in conversion the sudden transformation from the darkness of midnight to the brightness of noonday may so emphasize conversion that in after years a believer will look back with thanksgiving and longing to that period. The most progressive Christian will look with great joy to his entrance upon the Christian life, but after years of Christian service he knows that he is far in advance in grace and knowledge, in joy and peace, in consecration and anticipation, of what he was at the time of his initiation into the Christian life. The scarred veteran is better than the new recruit. The man who catches inspiration from the cannon's deep roar is better than he who trembles at the rifle's sharp crack. Paul saying, "I have a desire to depart and to be with

Christ," is a far greater man than Paul asking, "Lord, what wilt thou have me to do?"

Too many church-members are sulking in their tents instead of working or fighting in the field. Too many think the church is an ambulance to bear them to some spiritual retreat. Too many think the church is a hospital for the wounded rather than a school for learners, a vineyard for workers, and a battlefield for fighters. We are matriculated into the church as babes desiring the sincere milk of the word; we grow as strong men and women upon the strong meat of the word; and we are graduated that we may partake of angels' food in heaven. Growth and progress must be seen at every stage. I repeat, men have just as much religion as they desire to have; if they are satisfied with leanness they will be lean, but if they hunger and thirst after righteousness they will be filled. I can have no sympathy with men and women whose aim is to get something of heaven hereafter, and do as little as possible of God's will here and now. The true Christian never asks, is this or that duty or grace necessary to salvation? The man who strives to do as little as possible and to possess only such Christian graces as will not interfere with his worldly enjoyment, is guilty of the very climax of folly and meanness. The man who is determined to have only as much religion as will admit him to heaven is not likely to get nearer to heaven than he is in his half-hearted Christian life upon the earth.

What is heaven? To be like Jesus. Where is heaven? To be with Jesus. Every man has heaven here and now in proportion as he is like and with Jesus Christ. Heaven and hell hereafter are but the completed conditions of life on earth. The man who loves God cannot be kept out of heaven; he has heaven wherever he goes; the man who hates God cannot be kept out of hell, he has hell in himself. Heaven and hell are conditions as truly as they are places. No arbitrary allotment of God assigns men to heaven or to hell. They are the fruitage of the characters possessed during our earthly lives. No man will enter heaven at the last except heaven enter into him here. No man can be kept out of hell at the last except hell be gotten out of him here. There is tremendous solemnity in these great laws which sweep through the universe of God.

The differences which we see in Christian attainment are caused by the differences in the efforts made to make attainments in the Christian life. Our growth here will determine our standing hereafter. There are degrees in glory as truly as in punishment. No more certain is it that one star differeth from another star in glory, than that one man shall differ from another man in the resurrection of the dead. All who are Christians are saved by the precious blood of Christ alone; but great differences will be seen among the saved. Some are brought into the kingdom at the eleventh hour, plucked as brands from the burning; they are saved, yet so as by fire. There are others to whom an abundant entrance will be given, to whom the gates of glory will swing wide open; there are those who will enter with the shining train of the redeemed amid welcoming songs of saints and seraphs. Paul's heaven is very different from the heaven of the robber crucified with Jesus. All in heaven will be blessed, but the capacity for receiving blessing will differ greatly and will depend upon the spiritual development on earth. Some Christians are willing to remain babes in Christ; others earnestly strive to become perfect men in Christ.

Growth depends upon the use of appropriate means. There must first be spiritual life. No amount of tillage will cause a post which has been planted in the ground to grow as a tree. Culture may develop plants but never posts. Christ is the true source of life. No branch can bear fruit except it receive this life-giving sap from Christ, the living vine. There must be a foundation before a building can rise. There must be a candle, and it must be lighted before it can give light to all that are in the house. Growth implies and necessitates the existence of life; and there must be advancement or retrogression. A Christian is like a man on a bicycle, he must go on or soon go off. There can be no standing still for any length of time in the Christian race. The Christian race is either climbing or falling; it is either going up or down.

Among the means absolutely necessary to growth is the constant study of the word of God. Here are found to be the sincere milk for the young Christian and the strong meat for the mature believer. Here is found the bread of heaven, here the true hidden manna. The study of the word of God fits us for the work of God. The Bible is given that the man of God may be made perfect, thoroughly furnished unto all good works. Christ asked that his disciples might be sanctified through the truth, affirming in that connection "thy word is truth." As soldiers of God, part of our armor is to be the "sword of the Spirit, which is the word of God." Ignorance of the word of God accounts for the sickliness, feebleness, and the worthlessness of many church-members. Ignorance of God's word on the part of God's children is as lamentable as it is astounding. In order to Christian growth there must also be secret, family, and public prayer. The first step on the road away from Christ is usually taken in departing from the closet. Family prayer is much neglected in these busy, modern days. Constantine would have his statue representing him as kneeling in prayer. Only as men get down in lowliness before God can they go up in loftiness before men. The closet, where the soul meets alone with God, is the soul's banqueting room. A prayerful spirit will always find a time and place for prayer. Isaac found his place in the open field, David in his bedchamber, Daniel by the window, and Peter on the housetop. Only as men have power with God can they have power over their fellow-men. Prayer lays hold of the hand of Omnipotence and brings heaven down to earth. Well might Mary, queen of Scotland, say, "I fear the prayers of John Knox more than an army of ten thousand men." A praying church is the pulpit's strongest bulwark.

Growth in grace implies that we avoid secret sins. Jeremiah asks: "How long shall wicked thoughts harbor in thee?" We cannot always prevent the presence of evil thoughts, but we can help cherishing evil thoughts. We ought to know that if a man covets, he steals; if he hates, he murders. Secret defects in the Tay Bridge caused the terrific disaster when the thundering train reached the secretly weakened spans. No man is stronger than his weakest point, as no chain is than its weakest link. No man can long play the hypocrite. No man falls suddenly; he has long been leaning in the eye of God before he falls in the sight of men.

If you would grow in grace do not neglect the services of God's house. Much depends on constant attendance. Even one unnecessary absence may result in great harm. Thomas lost much by being absent from the evening assembly on the day of the resurrection. A week of agony, a spirit of unbelief, and an unreasonable demand of evidence resulted from that absence. Too many Christians are neglecting the evening service of God's house. They are giving aid and comfort to the enemies of the American Sunday. The Sunday is violently attacked on the outside, and many Christians are practically attacking it on the inside. Their conduct is disloyal to their church, dishonoring to their Lord, and unpatriotic toward their country.

That we may grow in grace and knowledge there must be on the part of all Christians labor for the conversion of others. Such labor is the first impulse of a redeemed soul. It is only the liberal soul that shall be made fat; it is only he that watereth others who may claim the promise that he himself shall be watered. We need a quenchless zeal, a glowing enthusiasm, and a Christly love for the salvation of those about us. Oh, for the zeal of consecrated laymen like Harlan Page, Uncle John Vassar, Dwight L. Moody!

There must be unwavering trust in God if there is to be growth in grace. He is able to keep that which we have committed unto him;

he will complete the work which he has begun. Only he who endures to the end shall be saved; only he who is faithful until death shall receive the crown of life. Never backslide. Never play the coward. Never deny the Lord who has bought you. It is the remark of Bunyan that, "they fall deepest into hell who fall backward." It is a terrible thing to fall from church-membership into an eternal hell. Beautiful is the story told of the brave Highland piper who was captured by Napoleon. He was told to play a march; he played it; to play an attack; he played it; to play a retreat, but the pipes gave forth no sound, he could only say, "I never learned that." O soldiers of Christ, do your duty. Stand firm, march bravely, attack fearlessly; die if you must, but, like the immortal Old Guard, never, never surrender.

VIII

THE EPHESIAN PRAYER

"For this cause I bow my knees unto the Father of our Lord Jesus Christ." Eph. 3 : 14-19.

VIII

FOR some time I have been studying the prayers of the Apostle Paul. They are a delightful subject for investigation, meditation, and discussion. It is deeply interesting to know that the Apostle Paul prayed for a church; it is still more instructive to know what are the blessings for which he prayed. What he prayed for, we may certainly pray for, both for ourselves and for the churches of Christ. His prayers would form a prayer-book which we might constantly study and daily use.

The prayer selected as the text this morning is unspeakably sublime. There is nothing of the nature of a prayer by any uninspired pen which can approach it for spirituality of feeling and for sublimity of language. There is nothing even in the Bible which can surpass it, perhaps no prayer or aspiration which can approach it, in the particulars named. The prayer bears a resemblance in important features to Solomon's great prayer at the dedication of the temple. In a certain sense the apostle was now dedicating the church of God; he, therefore, kneels down, as did Solomon, and invokes rich blessings which may abide in the spiritual temple of the Lord Christ. Every word of this prayer seems to have come direct from heaven; it is not of the earth earthy, but is heavenly in thought and divine in speech.

Paul's aspirations are God's inspirations. The matchless apostle piles word upon word in the endeavor adequately to express his great and glowing thoughts. He also adds intensive affixes to his words with the same object in view. The language is unparalleled in its sublimity. Dr. Adam Clarke has well said that no paraphrase can do the prayer justice, and that few commentators have entered into its spirit, probably being deterred by its loftiness of thought.

The "cause" for which he bows his knee, and to which he refers in the fourteenth verse, probably carries us back to the very first verse of the chapter, all between being regarded as a parenthesis. The apostle here prays to the Father, although the Lord Jesus by name is also addressed in prayer. He also prays with bowed knee. It has been said that "any posture but imposture" is appropriate in prayer. We know that the publican prayed standing and that his prayer was acceptable to God; but we know Daniel knelt when he prayed; that Stephen knelt when he prayed while the stones were falling upon him; that Peter knelt when he prayed, and said, "Tabitha, arise;" that Paul knelt while he prayed with and for the elders of the church at Ephesus who came to meet him at Miletus, and we know also that later they all "kneeled down on the shore and prayed."

Kneeling is the most natural, most reverent, and altogether appropriate attitude in prayer. Posture is not everything, but posture is something; posture is very much. We could scarcely forgive a man who could sit while presenting himself even to a human dignitary of whom he was asking a favor. There is authority in the Bible for praying either standing or kneeling, but none for praying while sitting in the presence of our Maker and Judge. It is most unfortunate that the habit of kneeling in prayer at public worship should have been discontinued; and it is to be hoped that it will soon be revived in all our churches. Because certain churches, whose errors Puritans felt bound to oppose, knelt in prayer in public worship, these Puritans felt called upon to oppose this attitude. Nothing but a narrow prejudice now prevents the general adoption of kneeling in prayer in the house of God. The denominations which affirm that they are always governed by apostolic example, ought to be the first to heed that example in their public prayers.

All the saints form one family. This family includes all true believers now upon the earth, the spirits of just men made perfect, and all the holy angels before the heavenly throne. It is instructive to emphasize the relation in the Greek words between father, "pater," and family, "patria," showing how this latter word is derived from the former. A true conception of the fatherhood of God results in a true conviction of the brotherhood of men. All God's children, whatever their color or creed, whether in this world or in distant spheres, are one family, and the day will come when they will stand together with holy rejoicing in the presence of their common Father.

We now see the blessings for which the apostle prays for this beloved church. The first petition, according to the sixteenth verse, is that they may have great spiritual strength. The source of all true strength, we are here taught, is God, and all spiritual blessings are divine gifts. The channel through which spiritual blessings come is the Holy Spirit, and the measure of spiritual blessing is "according to the riches of his glory," or according to his glorious riches. The measure of blessing is God's eternal fullness and infinite mercy. We may expect the measure of blessing to be according to his infinite ability. We do not expect a peasant to give as a millionaire might bestow. We need strength for daily duty in the glorious measure here indicated. We have enemies who are numerous and strong; we have grievous trials to bear; we have great temptations to overcome.

The location of this blessing is "in the inner man." Man consists of body, soul, and spirit. The inner man stands in special relations to God and the future life. As the outward man needs earthly food, so the inner man needs the bread of heaven. As truly as the body needs daily supplies, so does the soul its daily manna. Religion must have its normal support, or it will wither and decay. In the largest sense, Jesus Christ is the bread of life, of which we must eat. This is a glorious petition. We ought to offer it daily that we may grow in grace and in the knowledge of Jesus our Lord.

The next blessing asked for is the dwelling of Christ in our hearts. It has been supposed by some commentators that the apostle here likens the body, or the church, to a temple. We know that Solomon's temple was not complete until God honored it by his august presence. The church and each believer is to be "a holy temple in the Lord." Each Christian is to be "a habitation of God through the Spirit." Before man sinned he was God's temple; but when that temple was defiled by sin it was no longer a fit dwelling-place for deity. Christ comes to restore its pristine purity and to make it again a habitation for God. So the apostle prays, using terms in an intensive sense, that God may constantly dwell by faith in the hearts of his children. In the majestic passage in John 14: 23, our Lord said that on certain conditions regarding the believer, speaking of the Father and of himself, "We will come unto him and make our abode with him." That is truly a majestic "we." These are wonderful words; they are beyond the comprehension even of many who profess and call themselves Christians. Christ is the most desirable of all guests. Where his law of love dwells in human hearts, there he himself is in all the sweetness of his nature and in all the blessedness of his divine presence.

We learn also here that this indwelling in our hearts is by faith. Faith opens the heart's door to the coming of the Lord Jesus; faith sweetly invites him in and communes with him when he has taken up his residence in the soul. The language here employed is very strong; it might be rendered "that Christ may intensely and constantly dwell in our hearts"; it is almost impossible to transfer to English speech the intensive thought of the Greek words employed by the apostle. If the heart is not Christ's throne it must be Satan's seat. Which is it in your case to-day? Is it the abode of unclean spirits, or the dwelling-place of the Lord Jesus Christ? You can positively answer this question. Any man may know whether or not Christ dwells within him. Does Christ rule your life to-day? That is a plain question. What is your answer? I must press you to examine your heart and life in the presence of the omniscient God. Who dominates your will, self or Christ? With whom do you hold communion, Christ or Satan? In a word, are you Christ's freeman or Satan's dupe and slave? This is a question of the utmost importance. I beg that with Christ's help you will dethrone Satan and enthrone the Lord Jesus; receive him as your prophet to teach you, your priest to atone for you, and your king to command you.

We see by parts of verses seventeen, eighteen, and nineteen that the apostle prays that they may have an experimental knowledge of Christ's surpassing love. We are to understand that this is the love of Christ to them, not their love to him. We see also that in order to a possession of this knowledge they must be "rooted and grounded in love." We are here dealing with great truths and profound experiences. There is matter enough in this prayer for many sermons, matter enough for several volumes; but it is often of great importance that we take a considerable portion of Scripture as the basis of our exposition that we may catch the unity of its thought and the ultimate purpose sought by the writer. We know that love is the fulfilling of the law; we know that it is the fundamental principle of true religion. The apostle prays that they may be grounded in love. The love for which he prays is not an occasional emotion, but a continuous experience; it is not a sudden flash, but a steady flame.

He here employs two figures in very close relations in order that he may fully express his thought, but even his double metaphor is inadequate to his lofty purpose. He conceives of love as soil in which the Ephesian Christians were to strike their roots. They were to be as firm in Christ's love as a tree is in the soil when its roots go down deep and extend widely in all directions. This is the agricultural figure which the apostle employs; but immediately he introduces an architectural figure. His mind moved rapidly in the effort to express his grand conceptions. He multiplies and almost mixes his figures. The architect must have his ground plan and his minute specifications. As love is the soil in which Christian character is to grow, so love is the firm foundation on which the structure rests. Christians are to be grounded in love as a building is based on its foundation. On Christ's mighty love they were to rest as does a temple on the everlasting rock. Only when so rooted and grounded could they develop nobility of character and make great attainments in divine knowledge. It is interesting to observe that it is here suggested that there is a blessed companionship in this heavenly love. The Ephesian Christians were to comprehend the love "with all saints." Paul desired that all others might also appreciate the wonders of redemption. Christ's love is like the natural sun; each believer can have it all to himself without taking any portion from any other believer. The lowly plant can say to the sun, "thou art all mine"; and the lofty cedar can say, "thou art all mine." Sitting in my study, basking in the sunshine, I have as much thereof as if I were the only man in the universe.

We now come to the glorious dimensions of this love. We here reach wondrous heights, profound depths, and illimitable breadths. The love of God is measureless. Oceans and continents have been measured. The distance to the sun and stars from the earth is measurable; but the love of God is a sea without bottom or shore, is a universe without limits or dimensions. The language which the apostle employs in this part of the prayer is so full that it is impossible literally to translate it. His thought is that they may be thoroughly able fully to take in this mighty love. Intensive particles are constantly used in order to express his great thoughts. No angel's arithmetic can compute the vast dimensions of heavenly love. No algebraic formula can discover this unknown quantity—the greatness of Christ's love. Again some have supposed that there is a reference to the temple of God at Jerusalem, or possibly to the temple of Diana at Ephesus. We know that this latter temple was considered to be one of the wonders of the world. We know that by its length, breadth, and height, number of pillars, symmetry, and beauty it was worthy of the high esteem in which it was held. But if the apostle had any temple in view it is more natural to suppose that it was that at Jerusalem, which was built as the dwelling-place of God. It would suggest, and appropriately, the human heart as a temple and as the honored edifice in which deity might dwell. But it is not necessary to refer the language to any earthly building. It is simply the language of a heart surcharged with great thoughts and laboring to express them in forceful forms of speech. The apostle desires in the most emphatic manner to express his conception of Christ's love in redemption, and his own desire that the Ephesian church should in some way apprehend its greatness.

It is possible, however, for us to get additional suggestions from the apostle's descriptions of Christ's love. We know that imagination can but inadequately express or conceive these heavenly dimensions. They take in the eternity of God himself. God is love. In that definition there is an infinity of all dimensions, but our thought is helped by the apostle's descriptions. By the breadth of this love we may understand its reach to all ages and to all classes of sinners; its breadth is a girdle that surrounds the globe.

By its length we may understand its continuance from everlasting to everlasting; its vast reach from the eternal purpose in the mind of God to the eternal blessedness in the experience of the believer. By its depth we may understand its stooping to the lowest condition in our fallen race, to the deepest depravity of the most sinful soul. By its height we may understand the lofty altitude to which it raises men in their completed redemption; the infinite dignity which shall be theirs as sons of God and occupants of his throne.

The apostle prays that they may know the love of Christ which he immediately informs us passeth all knowledge. We have here a striking paradox; we are asked to know what surpasseth knowing. But the word "know" may be used in the sense of acknowledge or approve or experience. Although we may not know God fully, we may know him partially. But perhaps we ought simply to understand this extravagant language as the expression of a speaker whose heart was full to overflowing, and who, by the use of strong and even contradictory terms, is laboring to utter his profound and lofty thought. His mind reaches up to this infinite love. He knows much of its sweetness and preciousness. He wishes the Ephesian church to know it also. He struggles to rise to its great heights. Suddenly the truth flashes upon his mind that this is infinite love, that no one can fully know it, that no one can exhaustively tell it; that, like God, it is without beginning and without end, without measure and without limit. This love is a part of the science of salvation, the science of heaven, the science of the infinite God. It is unique love. There is nothing like it in the universe of God. Language utterly fails to tell its greatness. The Son of God plunged downward from the bosom of the Father to be the world's Redeemer. He became the child of the manger. He was the man of sorrows. He died on Calvary's cross. Was ever love like thine, thou Christ of God? It was love for bitterest foes. Such love cannot be told; but much of it may be known. A drop of the ocean tells something of the mighty deep. Oh, heavenly love! Oh, blessed paradox! Oh, wonderful prayer! May we know at least something of this surpassing love!

Lastly, the apostle prays that the Ephesian church might be filled with the fullness of God. This prayer abounds in great petitions, but this is the greatest of all. The best of the wine was kept for the last of the feast. Who can understand the glorious meaning of this petition? Perhaps the idea of the temple is still present in the apostle's mind. If so, he has spoken of its firm foundations and of its vast dimensions; but the glory of the temple is the indwelling of the deity to whose worship it is erected. The glory of the Lord filled the temple of Solomon. Paul's prayer now is that the Ephesian church may be filled with God. This is a remarkable petition; it is rich and glorious; it bewilders our judgment; it confounds our reasoning; it causes our imagination to reel, to wonder, to adore. It reminds us of Christ's majestic "we," as given in the passage in John to which we have referred; it reminds us of the exhortation that we should be holy as God is holy, and that we should be partakers of the divine nature. Not many believers are able to come up to the possibilities of this prayer. Some commentators have endeavored to weaken the force of the words by explaining that the apostle meant "so much of God's fullness as is communicable"; but we may be assured that the apostle knew the meaning of the petition which he offers. It is a great thing surely to pray that we should be full of God; greater still to be filled with the fullness of God; but unspeakably greater to pray that we be filled with all the fullness of God. We would not dare use such words if we had not the apostle's example as our authority. The word "fullness" is a favorite one with this apostle. It is a prayer that we should partake of all the fullness of the Eternal. Dare we offer this prayer? Dare we submit to the crucifixion of sin which it implies? Dare we grasp the thought of the

K

blessings which it includes? Dare we set bounds to the saving power and cleansing grace of the Almighty? Dare we offer this petition that we may receive its fullness of blessing?

We ought to pray this prayer oftener. Religion is everything. It is God's divinest gift to man. We live far below our possibilities as sons and daughters of the Almighty. We should be like God. We shall some day be like Christ, for we shall see him as he is. We shall live with him forever. We are here and now sons of God; we are here and now partakers of the divine nature. Here are dignity, nobility, grandeur, and glory. O men and women, admit Jesus Christ into your hearts to-day, and then all these blessings shall be yours for time and for eternity.

Sublimely does this chapter close with a doxology, a doxology which is in harmony with these glorious petitions; a doxology which recognizes that God is able to do all that we ask, and above all that we ask or even think. "Now unto him that is able to do exceeding abundantly above all that we ask or think, according to the power that worketh in us, unto him be glory in the church by Christ Jesus throughout all ages, world without end, Amen." Then let this doxology ascend to God, Father, Son, and Holy Spirit, in very truth, throughout all ages, world without end. Amen.

IX

THE ETERNAL PARADOX

"He that findeth his life shall lose it; and he that loseth his life for my sake shall find it." Matt. 10 : 39.

IX

TO the superficial reader the text is self-contradictory; to the careful thinker it is harmonious and sublime. It is the formulation of a universal and eternal law. The man who loves himself dies; the man who loves God supremely and his fellow-men rightly, lives here and will live in glory forever.

There is a sense in which all the higher truths are obscure and mystical, whether they are truths of science, art, or religion. Nature gives up her secrets only to her ardent worshipers; to see her beauties our eye must be trained; to hear her hidden harmonies our ear must be cultivated. To appreciate the Alps we must have mountains in our brains; to enjoy the sea we must have oceans in our soul. So to see God we must have the appropriate faculty—purity of heart; to understand his teaching we must have devotion to his will. They who do his will shall know his doctrine. The words of Christ were seed-thoughts, whose germination has only begun; much as they have developed they will develop vastly more in the ages to come.

We are indeed the "heirs of all the ages";

but the ages yet to come shall have a nobler heritage of truth for our heirs. Our fathers saw truth from afar and rejoiced; we touch the hem of her garment and find virtue in the touch. But our sons shall be admitted into her presence and commune with her forever. Christ spoke with a seeming obscurity because he could not speak otherwise. Earthly language can scarcely bear up under the weight of human thought; it breaks down utterly under God's thought. Christ packed away so much thought into his words that no one generation can get it all out. His words had a meaning for the simple men who first heard them and they are to have an ever-expanding meaning for all time. It is this fact which gives them their freshness, their charm, and their power. Their flower and aroma are constantly revealing themselves. The sayings of Christ open to us worlds of thought and feeling into which we may enter, but which are too full to be emptied of all their treasures by human hearts and minds. Our text is one of these suggestive germinal truths. It is an epitome of the wisdom and history of the past; and it is a prophecy of the wisdom and history of the future. It furnishes the crucial test of character, and explains the secret of true greatness. I shall endeavor to illustrate both sides of the truth here presented in the order in which they are given.

First, then, how can it be averred with truth that "He that findeth his life shall lose it"? A fuller interpretation of the word life will clarify our ideas of the possibility of finding it and of losing it, and will also reduce the seeming contradiction to perfect harmony. As we have hinted, Jesus uses here the same word in two different senses. The first refers to the natural, physical, lower life; the second to the higher, nobler, spiritual life. In an earlier verse, Jesus uses the word soul, life, as something distinct from our physical life; in the text he passes from one meaning to the other. The idea is, "He that is bound up in himself, in saving his earthly life, shall lose his spiritual life; but he who in his devotion to Christ is willing to imperil, to destroy, to crucify his lower life shall save his higher life. The truth here taught goes to the very center of being, and it strikes at our inmost self. Christ's words are thus directed against every form of selfishness. They teach us that he who loses his mortal life in the service of Christ shall save his immortal life—if I may so speak. And this immortal life is to be enjoyed now, for the contrast is not between the present life and the future life,—the words of comparison being used in the past tense,—but between the outward, secular, earthly life, and the inward, spiritual, eternal life which commences on earth and will be perfected in heaven. The man who has not lost himself to this lower life is dead even now, and the man who has found himself in Christ has this higher life even now.

Christ teaches us that to live is more than to be. Mere being is only the animal side of living; but true living is the Godlike side of being. Those who heard these pregnant words from the lips of Jesus were to be prepared for his sake to give up their bodily lives; his reference to the cross shows that he had that possibility in mind. In our day the words have a somewhat different application. We are not called upon to give up our lives as martyrs; but we are called upon to give up the sinful self-life of the old man, which is truly death, and which is to be lost by an internal and continual crucifixion, in order that we may find our true life both here and hereafter. To lose life, then, in the application of the sense of the text to ourselves, is to lose our sinful self. To lose self is to lose sin, and sin, when finished, is death. This explanation harmonizes the text with itself and with all our experience.

All the principles of action among men may be reducible to two. The first is that of Satan and Cain; the second is that of Christ and Paul. The first in Satan exalts self above all that is called God; and in Cain it sneeringly asks, "Am I my brother's keeper?" The second in Christ says, "Not my will but thine be done," and in Paul, "I count not my life dear unto me"; and in both Christ and Paul loses its life that others may find life. We are all to-day obeying one or the other of these principles. Our only hope, as individuals and churches, is that we shall follow, here and everywhere, in the footsteps of Christ. Our prayer should be that we may be lifted out of this low, sinful, dying, self-life into the high and holy and Christly life of him who is the way, the truth, and the life.

Permit me also briefly to illustrate the other side of my text: "He that loseth his life for my sake shall find it." If it be true that selfishness is the essence of sin, and that sin is death, that loving our lower life begets the disease which corrupts, and finally the canker which destroys the soul's true life, then the opposite of this—self-abnegation—must produce opposite effects. True living must be in our loving God and our fellow-men, laboring "together with God" for their good. This truth Jesus taught in his works, his words, and his death. His life was an illustration of and a commentary on my text. His was a life of self-sacrifice. He lives now, the mightiest force in the world's thought, because once he gave his life for the world's sin. He is the world's Prophet, Priest, and King, because once he died as the world's sacrifice. Never did kingly crown betoken such royalty or demand and receive such homage as Christ's crown of thorns. He was maligned, mocked, murdered; but no one ever charged him with living for himself. His enemies sneeringly said, "He saved others; himself he cannot save." His complete self-abnegation is marvelous. He had no self-life. He knew himself only as obedient to God and ministrant to man. His life is so blended with that of his Father that he could say, "He that believeth on me believeth not on me, but on him that sent me"; and yet in his consciousness of personality he could triumphantly say, I lay down my life, and take it up again—no man taketh it from me.

Those who have taken in the meaning of Christ's life, who at his cross have kindled their hearts with his love, and who by daily communion with their risen Lord have kept the flame burning, are the men and the women who are to win the world to Christ. God knows men, and with a justice unwavering and a wisdom unerring he rewards them. The law of my text is universal as gravitation, and eternal as God. It is not an arbitrary enactment, but the revelation of an eternal principle. If we put ourselves in line with it by coming as helpless sinners to Jesus, losing at his cross our poor, sinful, selfish, lower life, we shall find our higher life here and eternal glory hereafter. If we refuse, and cling to our dying life we must die now, and we shall die the second death hereafter.

And as Christ was thus obedient to the will of

God, so Paul was obedient to the will of Christ, and could say, "I live, yet not I, but Christ liveth in me." He lost himself in his devotion to Christ, and yet he stands more conspicuously before the world than any other man. No personality is more unique, none so imperishable, as that of Paul. He counted not his life dear unto him; he was willing to give it up—he did give it up—for Christ; he lost himself in Christ, and losing himself he found a life which the Christian world will cherish forever. And all of us who have met great temptations and who have overcome them through him who has loved us and given himself for us, have learned that in losing ourselves at the altar of Christ we have found our nobler life. When a man first learns that he is a child of God through faith in Jesus, that he has gone out of his old, sinful self-life into that of God, a thrill of intenser being, such as he never knew before, fills his soul. Such a man sees God in everything and everything in God. He loses all dread of eternity; God and eternity are in him and he in them. A great love which puts a man into sympathy with other hearts reproduces in him something of the life and love of all those with whom he thus sympathizes; and the greater the extension of his love the greater will be the *intension* of this life. It was thus that Christ could taste death for every man, for his life took in that of every man.

Profoundly he is to be pitied who has never known a love which has enabled him to enter into and partake of another's life; unspeakably happy is he who has so entered into and partaken of the life of Christ; for he who has fellowship with him in his sufferings, shall have kinship with him in his triumphs. The highest life, like Christ's, is always the most unconscious life. Let us remember that Christ, in giving us such a principle as my text contains, is not forcing upon us an arbitrary rule; he is merely revealing the universal law of life. It is not true simply because he uttered it; but, more strictly speaking, he uttered it because it is true. The geologist does not make the laws of his science; he reveals them. This law existed before Christ came, and would exist had he never come; he merely revealed it. With this law conform the lives of all men who have become truly great. They did their work, they thought not of themselves. They were willing to be lost, and God found them. When the tide of public feeling turned against Socrates, all his pupils left him but one. A sophist twittingly said, "Ha! Socrates, your reputation has gone, you have but one pupil." "Yes," said he, "but that one is Plato." Day by day he walked the groves and taught his pupil, and that pupil, by the influence of his writings, has made Socrates walk through the world as a teacher ever since.

He was willing to lose not only his pupils, but his life, in support of the truths he taught; and no sooner was he dead than he began to live in the world's history. He lost his life; he found a higher life. I do not endorse him in all his life; but, heathen though he was, he illustrates the truth of my text.

This principle is illustrated in the case of Savonarola, the Florentine friar, whose aim was to glorify Christ and to purify the Roman Church. He died a martyr, but his death was his life; it made him immortal, and being dead, he spoke from his grave to Martin Luther and other Reformers, cheering them on to victory. Twenty years after his death, Raphael painted his portrait, and it was placed among the saints in the halls of the Vatican. In 1789 all England was astonished when Wilberforce delivered his great speech on the slave trade. Burke declared that he was not surpassed by any of the great orators of Greece or Rome. But his friends mourned over the position which he had taken; it would estrange his warmest supporters, destroy his fair reputation, and blast his promising career. The brilliant young man who dazzled Paris and delighted England with his wit and wisdom was in his self-sacrificing course a mystery to all. But there is an explanation. At the age of twelve he learned at the house of a Methodist aunt something of Jesus and his love. The gayety of the

French court, the flattery of admirers, and the consciousness of triumph, did not obliterate these thoughts. Conscience was continually active; and finally he felt himself to be a lost sinner. Then he saw the Lamb of God who taketh away the sin of the world. At the cross of Christ he found peace in believing. There he lost himself in the will of Christ, and there he determined that if he took part in the government of Great Britain it would be as a servant of Jesus Christ. On Sunday, the 28th of October, 1787, he wrote these words in his journal: "God Almighty has set before me two great objects—the suppression of the slave trade, and the reformation of manners." He knew the difficulties before him. "But then," said he, "we have God and Christ on our side, the crown is everlasting life, and the struggle short compared with eternity." The love of Christ was his inspiration. Could the astonished members of Parliament, in 1789, who heard him speak and saw him vote have looked into that room where two years before he laid his life, his hopes and fears, his defeats and triumphs, on the altar of Christ, they would have learned the secret of his power and the motive of his life. He lost himself; God found him, the world has honored, and eternity will glorify him.

The text finds its illustration not only in the great events of life, but also in the ordinary routine of duties when performed in the Spirit of Christ. The young man who, in a little homely meeting-house in Boston, on a wet and cheerless evening in October, 1823, preached to a few shivering people a sermon which the next morning he confessed to have been an utter failure, saying it fell perfectly dead, was finding himself when he little dreamed of such a result. A thoughtful deacon had the sermon published. It soon ran through several editions. A leading Presbyterian highly praised it, and Robert Hall on reading it predicted a brilliant future for its author. Its subject was "The Moral Dignity of the Missionary Enterprise." That sermon made Francis Wayland president of Brown University, and that presidency made him his country's Wayland.

Often in morals, as in science, we are obliged to reason back from the facts to the law governing the facts. In this way, from our observations of life, we might have discovered some such law as that stated in the text. For we know well that when a man deliberately proposes self as the object of his worship it is not difficult to foresee the result. Such worship degrades the man, doing violence to all his nobler instincts and aspirations. Such a man sinks from love into hate, from life into death. Thus the fearful and inevitable penalty of seeking self ends, directly in harmony with the fundamental law of life, in losing self. This is also its indirect result. Outside influences co-operate with the laws of being in bringing about this result. Society is suspicious of such men. It watches them, combines against them, overthrows their best-laid plans, defeats their projects, and gives to others the prizes which they fondly hoped to win. Novelists teach a great truth when they make villainy fail of its end, just because of the villainous means by which it hoped to gain its end. God is neither asleep nor on a journey, and he will most effectively thwart the selfish by permitting them to fall into their own snares.

History illustrates and corroborates this truth. Never had a man a grander opportunity for doing grandly than had Pilate. Never did a man fail so fatally. Never before might justice have appeared so just; never wickedness so wicked. His was a great part to act; it might have been sublime; it was unspeakably base. He sat on the throne of power when he who had all power was weak before him; he was judging him who was the Judge of the quick and the dead. One scarcely dares think of the awful possibilities and destinies of time and eternity which hung on the actions of Pilate. We may not presume to go too far into these awful mysteries; but this we do know, Pilate ought to have done right. He was so disposed at the first. He knew little and he cared less about the annoying questions of these annoying Jews. Christ is to him at worst but a wild enthusiast, he finds him innocent of any crime; he will set him free. But Jewish hatred to Christ will not be baffled so easily. Priestly cunning will arouse self in Pilate, and thus accomplish its end. "If thou let this man go, thou art not Cæsar's friend." Pilate was an ambitious politician; the question is now no longer one of right. It is position, power, self, on the one side; justice, truth, Christ, on the other side. Self Pilate loved; self he was determined to find; he therefore slew Christ. His hands he might wash in the sight of the multitude from the blood of Christ, but his soul in the sight of heaven he could not wash from the sin of slaying the Holy One. He should have remembered the grand Roman motto, "Let justice rule though the heavens fall"; he should have made it impossible for the Jews to take Jesus. I do not judge Pilate by the Christian standard; such a judgment would be manifestly unjust. I judge him merely by the Roman law, which he was bound to execute; and by that law, according to his own confession, I condemn him.

But did Pilate gain his object? Did he cheat God? Did he falsify my text? To conciliate the Jews, and thereby retain his position, he violated every principle of right, and God made those very Jews his instruments in punishing Pilate, charging him with crimes before the home government, and depriving him of the very office to retain which he sacrificed all justice. And Pilate in his lonely banishment in Gaul, finally taking his life with his own hand, losing himself with an eternal loss, is a fitting sequel to Pilate finding himself at the sacrifice of eternal rectitude. It is an awful crisis in a man's life when he must, as we all must at some time, decide between self and Christ. God help us all to do right when these great decisions are to be made!

"He that findeth his life shall lose it" was literally fulfilled in the case of Archbishop Cranmer. He confessed Christ against the devil and the pope; and as a reward for his loyalty to truth he was ordered to be burned. Then in the hour of trial the flesh became weak; the lower life asserted itself over the higher; he recanted. But notwithstanding that he signed six recantations nothing short of his death would satisfy his foes and he was burned on March 21, 1556. The hand that signed the recantation he held in the flames to be burned first, as an atonement for its baseness; and that shriveled hand seems still to point with warning finger to the words, "He that saveth his life shall lose it."

These illustrations might be greatly multiplied. The pages both of profane and sacred history are blotted over with the names of those who to save self became traitors to their country, their souls, and their God, those who, to enjoy the pleasures of sin for a season, sacrificed on the altar of self all that is noble in manhood and glorious in immortality. Looking at their folly and wickedness one might speak harshly; but remembering that we all find in our own hearts so much of self and sin, our severity gives place to pity and our pride to prayer.

God be thanked, this finding is not limited to those whose loss for Christ is conspicuous before the world. Those sweet and gentle natures, who come like angels of God to earth, and then pass away before their work seems half-done, have not lived in vain. A man's infirmity is often his power. You remember Kirke White's plaintive song: "I shall die and be forgotten, and the world will go on as if I had never been; and yet how have I loved, how have I longed, how have I aspired!" We feel to-day the impulse of his brief life, and poetry catches new inspiration at his grave. And all that host of unknown men and women whose presence has filled the world with blessing, though their hallowed names may not like Howard's be mentioned in the households of the world; those quiet, patient wives and mothers whose tears are now jewels, and whose groans are angelic music; all those who loved Christ and labored for him, in however humble a capacity, while their eyes grew brighter, their cheeks paler, and their hearts purer, until they laid aside the veil of flesh and gently passed away—God holds them in everlasting remembrance.

Do we talk of our losses for Christ? Compared with his cross, what is ours? Compared with his sacrifice we shall be ashamed to mention ours. There is no corner sufficiently obscure to hide a man who has zeal to work, patience to wait, and faith to pray. The world wants such men, and it will find them. God wants such men, and he reaches out his hand to them and says, "Come up higher." The quiet, faithful, self-sacrificing men and women who are willing to lose themselves for Christ are those who do the work for Christ in the world. To those who seek first the kingdom of God and his righteousness will be added all other things. O men and women, give yourselves to God. Lay your poor, weak lives at his feet; let him take your sinful hearts that he may make them his temple. Let this lower, earthly, sinful self die with Christ on the cross; then you shall live to walk here with Christ in newness of life and forever with him in the bliss of heaven.

X

THE GRATEFUL EXHORTATION

"And let us arise and go up to Bethel, and I will make there an altar unto God, who answered me in the days of my distress and was with me in the way which I went." Gen. 35 : 3.

X

JACOB and his mother plotted wickedly against Isaac and Esau. Jacob early manifested the retiring character of his father, preferring the quiet life of the shepherd rather than the daring pursuits of the hunter, which so fascinated his brother Esau. Jacob early became Rebekah's favorite, while for Esau Isaac evinced marked partiality. Jacob showed a prudent, and, perhaps, we might say, a selfish and cunning spirit even in his youth. The manner in which he secured the honor of the birthright from his brother Esau was as cunning in execution as it was selfish in design. The favoritism shown him by his mother proved to be greatly hurtful rather than helpful in his history and character. Nothing can justify the deception practised by Rebekah and Jacob. It is true that God had promised that the elder should serve the younger; but God never requires our sinful acts to enable him to fulfill his divine promises. The conduct of the mother and son in plotting against the father and the other son presents a truly painful picture. Justification of such conduct is simply impossible We do not feel called upon to utter one word in extenuation of the guilt of either mother or son. True religion is not responsible for Jacob's conduct, for at this time he did not have true religion. His conversion, as we use the term in later days, did not occur until the night of his profound experiences on the bank of the brook Jabbok. Some have tried to excuse the acquisition of his father's blessing on the ground that the whole history is simply figurative and symbolic; but so to explain the transaction is to blunder exegetically as much as the attempt to justify the deceit would be to blunder morally.

Punishment soon followed the committal of the sin. Jacob was filled with alarm, and at his mother's suggestion was sent to Mesopotamia, the seat of her family, in order that he might find a wife among his own kindred, and also to escape the consequences of his brother's anger. The marriage of Esau to Hittite women doubtless gave the parents greater anxiety for the proper marriage of Jacob. Once more Jacob received his father's blessing, and then started upon his journey. The years pass and his return was now contemplated.

During this time he had grown rich and " increased exceedingly and had much cattle, and maidservants and menservants, and camels and asses." But the time had now come when the Lord wished him to return to his own country. The voice of God, therefore, came to him saying, " Arise, go up to Bethel, and dwell there." This command was in harmony with the desires alike of Jacob and his family. They started on their journey, and the prosperity and departure of Jacob grieved and angered Laban. On the third day after their departure, Laban learned that they had gone and immediately set out in pursuit ; but he was divinely warned not to hinder Jacob's return. Reproach and recrimination were freely indulged in on both sides. Crafty men and craftier women practised their various arts upon one another for their selfish ends. Rachel stole the teraphim which Laban was so anxious to discover and to preserve ; and the theft soon necessitated further deceit. Jacob's reply, however, was manly and just ; but it showed how imperfectly they all were instructed in the law of God in moral duty. Peace finally was restored, and Laban returned, while Jacob and his family continued their journey. A heap of stones, called Mizpah, a watch-tower, was built as a witness between these warring and distrustful men. The first use of the word Mizpah robs it of much of the beauty and poetry associated with the word in our day. Its primary use was to keep a check upon two sharpers, neither of whom dared to trust the other. It was diamond cut diamond when these two wily men transacted business with each other.

Then came the skillful preparations to meet Esau. Jacob relied upon two great weapons—

"brains and prayer." He divided his flocks and herds into two companies, so that if one were attacked, the other might escape. Then came the great crisis in his life—the meeting of the angel on the banks of Jabbok. Then Jacob was converted; then the old name and nature suggested by Jacob, the supplanter, were exchanged for Israel, the prince and soldier of God. After this night of anxiety and triumph Jacob rose from Peniel with the bright sun shining upon him as an emblem of the radiant hope which illuminated his own soul. Finally at Shalem, a city of Shechem in the land of Canaan, he pitched his tent. Sorrow came to his life, because of the sin and shame of his family. He was now an old man and his heart was bowed with domestic grief, but God's eye and God's love were still upon him, and God's voice was heard commanding him to go to Bethel and dwell there. Then Jacob gave the exhortation to his family in our text.

1. In studying this text, we have, in the first place, *an exhortation*—"And let us arise, and go up to Bethel." This exhortation possesses many interesting features. It will pay us to study for a little time some of its characteristics. It was an exhortation given by the command of God. By the first verse of this chapter we see that God said, "Arise, go up to Bethel, and dwell there." Jacob had now been some time in the

land. His life was partly pastoral and partly agricultural. He was engaged in the care of his family and in the feeding of his flocks. His sons had involved him in painful difficulties, and his daughter's sorrow had brought him intense grief and shame. His great herds required constant attendance. There was ground for fearing that the cares of this world and the deceitfulness of riches would choke the good seed which had been sown in his heart. Since that wonderful night at the ford of Jabbok we find less imperfection and more for commendation in his life and character; but we certainly do not yet find freedom from weakness and perfection of character. He seems already in danger of forgetting God; he seems in danger of forgetting that his name is Israel, and lapsing again into the old and hateful Jacob character. But his family troubles and the opposition of the people about him are likely to lead him nearer to God. At this critical time God speaks and tells him to go up to Bethel, and make there an altar. It is always cause for gratitude when God speaks to his children as they are in danger of wandering into sin; it is always a proof of divine sonship when we are willing to listen to God's voice and to walk in the way of his commandments. We can have no evidence for ourselves or for others that we are truly the children of God except as we are led by the Spirit of God. The dutiful spirit proves our adoption into God's family.

Another characteristic of this exhortation is that it is given by the head of a household to his family. This truth is taught us in the verse that precedes the text; we are there told that Jacob spoke unto his household. This fact is profoundly suggestive. Every father should be the religious head of his own house; every father should be the high priest in his own family. He should be unwilling to give up the high honor and sacred duty which belong to him as the head of his house. He ought to erect the family altar and constantly to keep the flame of family devotion brightly burning thereon. Jacob was regarded by his family as in some sense a prince and a priest; so ought every father to regard himself and to be regarded by others. The sacred duty of ministering at the family altar he cannot neglect or ever remit without dishonoring himself as well as his Lord. Jacob commanded his family to put away all strange gods that were among them, to change their garments, and to be themselves clean. Some of his family had their hands full of blood; they needed not only clean clothes and hands, but also clean hearts. His family seem to have responded to this earnest exhortation. It is blessed when the head of the home leads in paths of obedience to God, and when the family with alacrity and joy follows in his footsteps. It is unspeakably sad to see families sit at tables on which no blessing is asked, and live in houses in which the voice of praise and prayer is never heard. Almost as well might a family live in a house without a roof as in a house in which the presence of God is not recognized. Jacob's example at this point is worthy of earnest commendation and of universal imitation.

It was also an exhortation to attend the house of God. This is the meaning of the word Bethel. We are carried back at once to the account given in the twenty-eighth chapter of this book, of Jacob's flight from home and his night spent at Bethel. At that time Jacob was a wanderer fleeing from the voice of his angry brother. He carried with him the heaviest of all burdens for a traveler, a guilty conscience. He is in a lonely place as night comes down upon him. He is weary and sinful and sad. He is on a ridge which has been called the backbone of Palestine. He must go on foot and alone a distance of hundreds of miles through an inhospitable country. If he had possessions he would be robbed; but without money he must beg. It will take him a month to make the journey. It has been pointed out that the journey was longer than that of Washington from Virginia to Fort Duquesne, for the performance of which he received the admiration of the civilized world. About him on this ridge stand and lie huge masses of stone in confused heaps. He is an outcast in a howling wilderness. The darkness deepens. In his loneliness he feels the need of the divine presence and sympathy as perhaps he never felt it in his father's tent. He sleeps; he dreams. The rough stones which he saw as he was closing his eyes in slumber become in his dreams a golden stairway leading to heaven; up and down this terraced steep pass the messengers of God. He watches; he wonders. These messengers are now in the dazzling splendors of God's glory, and God's voice is heard renewing the promise of mercy and of countless blessings. The morning dawns, and the astonished sleeper awakens, and his soul is filled with holy awe. In his surprise and wonder he expresses his joy, and also reveals his imperfect ideas of the Deity by saying, "Surely the Lord is in this place, and I knew it not." To him this place became the house of God and the gate of heaven. The stone which was his pillow he anoints with oil, and calls it and the place Bethel. Perhaps it was some rough monument, more like the cairns seen in Wales and Scotland than a single stone. We know that in many countries such stones are still selected as the monuments of great events. These rude stones were hints at least of the great ecclesiastical edifices of later days; it was an anticipation of all the lowly chapels and lofty cathedrals of subsequent times. The name Bethel has been transformed and used by Phœnicians and Mohammedans with sacred associations, as with Jews and Christians. Jacob's language showed that he had ill-defined notions of God. He would make bargains with God even as with Esau, and later with Laban.

This, then, is a father's exhortation to his family to attend the house of God. It is an exhortation which is appropriate still. It is an exhortation which is forgotten too often. Sunday is to many a day of listless indifference or of unholy pleasure. Are we to have a continental Sunday in our beloved land? This is at this moment a practical question. Many Christians are largely responsible, by their indifference to the claims of God's day and God's house, for the general neglect of that day and house on the part of men of the world. Many Christians will lazily spend their morning or evening, or both, in their own homes instead of meeting with God's people in God's house. Parents, let me exhort you to follow Jacob's example. Employers, let me ask you, where are your clerks and employees to-day? Have you ever followed Jacob's example in exhorting your households to go up to Bethel? Do you set them this noble example yourself? Put away the strange gods of dishonesty, of unfairness, and of impurity, from offices and stores, from homes and hearts, and then urge all under your influence to go with you up to Bethel. Determine to-day that as for you and your house you will serve the Lord.

2. We also have here *a solemn vow*—" I will make there an altar unto God." Jacob would there renew his vow made at Bethel, that if God would keep him in the way and bring him again to his father's house, the Lord should be his God. This is, of course, a very mercenary view to take of one's duty to God; but Jacob at that time was not capable of taking any higher view. God kept his part of the contract, although Jacob's motive therein was neither manly nor godly. Jacob had now been some time in the land of his fathers, but until now his vow was neglected. It is well that it is remembered now. Have not we like him often forgotten our vows? Amid the anxiety and frivolity of life we have often forgotten the vows we made to God in the day of trouble. In time of business disasters and of family griefs, in times of sickness and on beds of languishing, we have made solemn vows to God; but we must with shame confess that when health and vigor were returned the vows were forgotten. Your good resolutions vanished like the morning cloud and the early dew. You made vows of service to God at the waters of baptism, at the table of Communion, and audibly in the presence of his people at the covenant meeting. Perhaps you have been away from the city and many of

these vows have been neglected. Perhaps to-day the memory of broken vows heavily oppresses your mind and heart. What shall you do? Give way to discouragement and despair? A thousand times, no! Come back again to the neglected altar, to the forgotten cross, and to the despised Redeemer. Pray with the publican, "God be merciful to me a sinner," and you shall assuredly go down to your house justified.

We notice also that Jacob promised to make there an altar unto God. In his wanderings it is to be feared that his altars had been often neglected. They were broken down and God was forgotten. Now he is once more in the land of Canaan, the land of his fathers; now he is going up to Bethel, the house of his God; and now he promises to make there an altar unto his God. This is a wholesome resolution on the part of Jacob; it gives us a ground for hope that he will be worthy of the noble name of Israel. It is to be feared that often business duties and family cares so press upon God's people that their family altar is neglected. This church is in a certain sense your Bethel. Here in your heart now erect the altar, and then at your home let the voice of prayer be heard; let God be acknowledged and his peace will certainly be enjoyed. If any family altars have fallen down, let them be rebuilt. Has the altar of private and secret prayer been neglected? Should we trace the history of all those who have dishonored their profession and have wandered from their church, it would be found in the majority of instances, that the first step in the downward way was taken when they neglected the place of secret prayer. To be strong among men we must receive strength when alone with God. We need for the development of character times of quiet study of the Scriptures and of secret communion with God. There is much less of earnest meditation on divine things than our spiritual growth demands. Our Lord commanded us to enter into the closet. Have you all secret Bethels, some place where God has met with you, and where you often meet with him? No matter where this place may be, if only God be there it shall be a Bethel indeed. Christ often found a secret place of prayer on the lonely mountain. Isaac found a place of meditation in the field. Peter and other disciples found a Bethel on the housetops. I read the other day of a chimney sweep, who said that his closet was in the chimney when hidden from human eye. We remember that Dr. Payson said: "As soon as I began, when a student, to beg God's blessing on my studies, I did more in one week than in a whole year before." Luther, when most pressed with his enormous tasks, said: "I have so much to do that I cannot get on without three hours a day of praying." We know that General Havelock rose at four, when he had to begin with the march at six, in order to enjoy the privilege of secret communion with God before entering on the duties of the day. Devout heathen have set us an example which many professed Christians might follow for themselves. It is said that Pericles, the great Athenian statesman, never addressed an audience without praying to the gods for help; and that Scipio never undertook an affair of importance without spending some time alone in some temple of the gods. Have any of your family altars fallen? Are there any families in which they have never been built? Abraham built his altar wherever he pitched his tent. Lot pitched his tent, but we do not read that he built his altar. The Canaanites looked on in wonder while the noble Abraham recognized his God.

Social prayer has been too much neglected. The prayer meeting is the place of power in a church. Well might Queen Mary say: "I fear the prayers of John Knox more than an army of ten thousand men." Well might the gifted and now glorified Tennyson sing:

> More things are wrought by prayer
> Than this world dreams of. Wherefore let my voice
> Rise like a fountain for me night and day.
> For what are men better than sheep or goats
> That nourish a blind life within the brain,
> If, knowing God, they lift not hands of prayer
> Both for themselves and those who call them friend?

> For so the whole round world is every way
> Bound by gold chains around the feet of God.

Resolve to-day in the presence of God and his people that like Jacob you will build an altar unto God.

3. We have in this text, in the last place, a *sufficient reason for the exhortation given and the promise made*—"Who answered me in the day of my distress, and was with me in the way which I went." We have already seen that Jacob had many causes for gratitude. His gratitude is seen in the prayer he offers as he goes out to meet Esau. There he recognizes his unworthiness before God; there he acknowledges God's many gifts toward him, saying: "For with my staff I passed over this Jordan, and now I am become two bands." Things went prosperously with him in his sojourn with Laban. He was more than a match for Laban in ingenuity and industry. God had fulfilled the promise which he had made to him at Bethel. So God has been gracious to us. At times we have been brought low, and then he helped us, as he did the psalmist. Often the psalmist appeals to his past as the ground for present trust and future hope. He sings: "I love the Lord, because he hath heard my voice and my supplications . . . therefore will I call upon him as long as I live." Trust God in the future because he has helped you in the past. Let your yesterdays of blessings be

the prophets of your to-morrows of assurance. Is it dark with you to-day? Was it not darker with you some other day, and yet God delivered you and illuminated your path? Jacob was troubled now, but would not the God of Bethel and Jabbok be his God still? Surely God was with him in the day of his distress and in the way which he went. Surely God has been with you more really than with Jacob. Away then with your fears. Take no counsel of your doubts. There is brightness in the future. Courage, brother, sister, friend. Build your altar now unto God and lay yourself joyfully as a living sacrifice thereon. The God who answered in the past answers still. In that night vision God promised to be with Jacob; this promise he renewed when Laban would take advantage of Jacob. All through his checkered career God was with him; God would not leave him in the trials awaiting him. His mother, who so loved him, was no more. To help him she sinned, and she probably never saw him again. His beloved Rachel was soon to give her life in giving life to him whom with her departing breath, she called Benoni, but whom Jacob called Benjamin. Isaac too had died, and soon Jacob must sorrow over the deception of his sons and the loss, as he thinks, of Joseph and Benjamin. But the sunset of his life was calm, bright, and beautiful. After seventeen years in the land of Goshen enjoying serene happiness, he gave his dying blessing in Jehovah's name to his assembled sons, and then at the age of one hundred and forty-seven years was gathered to his fathers. His body was embalmed, and finally buried with great honor in the burial place of Abraham near Hebron.

Has not God been with us in the way which we went? Was not God with us during the past year, preserving our country from disaster, from plague, and from pestilence? Oh, how good God is to us, to our families, and to our church! Let your hearts to-day overflow with gratitude, and let your lives be consecrated afresh to his service. Let us not waste time in useless repining over misspent hours, wasted opportunities, and personal sorrow; let us gird ourselves now for fresh conflicts and for noble victories. Are we to-day pure in heart, more Christlike in life than we were a year ago? God help us to do our whole duty in our business circles, in our domestic relations, and in our church life! Let each one now make these resolutions his own in harmony with the teaching of the text:

"I will attend the house of God; I will make an altar of prayer; I will cherish gratitude to God; I will give my heart to God, and devote my life to him who was with me in the way which I went."

XI

THE AUTHORITATIVE EVIDENCE

"Hereby know we that we dwell in him." 1 John 4 : 13.

XI

MANY earnest Christians are often in doubt as to the reality of their conversion. At times they ask with an earnestness bordering on agony, "Have we ever truly experienced the regenerating grace of God?" The language of the hymn formerly often sung, "Am I his or am I not?" has frequently been the question of many a devout, but doubting, Christian. It is certainly deeply interesting and equally profitable to be able to give an inspired answer to so important a question; and it is still more interesting to give this answer in the words of so competent a judge as the Apostle John. I shall, at this time, in answering this question, confine my replies to the words of the beloved disciple, and I shall arrange his answers in their logical order. He loved to speak of the new birth. This and related forms of expression were familiar phrases on his lips and pen. He learned this language from the lips of the heavenly Teacher; and especially from the definite instructions on this point given him, perhaps by Jesus himself, when reporting the nocturnal interview with Nicodemus. We have then for our subject authoritative proofs of conversion, as given by the beloved disciple. He sets forth most clearly in a series of statements in his First Epistle, the distinguishing characteristics of true believers. Hereby know we that we dwell in him. He teaches us that a true Christian is a believer in our Lord Jesus Christ—" Whosoever believeth that Jesus is the Christ is born of God" (1 John 5 : 1). We must not suppose that the apostle means to say that mere intellectual assent to the bare proposition that Jesus is the Messiah, the anointed of God, is evidence of regeneration. We suppose that he means to affirm that this truth must be so believed as to produce its legitimate effect on the life. We have no evidence that a man has believed truly in Christ except he live a Christly life. The apostle means to teach that we are to accept Christ as the Messiah of prophecy in the Old Testament and of history in the New Testament.

True faith in Jesus Christ is not merely assent of the head; it includes also the consent of the heart. We know that those who have never been born again may give an intellectual assent to the proposition that Jesus is the Christ. When he was upon the earth many demons believed in him in some sense as their master. Devils are represented in Scripture as doing so now, and as trembling before his power. But true faith implies a consciousness of sin, a deserving of wrath, and a believing with the heart in Christ as the only Saviour. True faith is a looking to and trusting in the righteousness of Christ for justification; true faith lays hold of his atoning sacrifice for the pardon of sin and for peace with God; true faith is the acceptance of Christ as the only hope for salvation for time and for eternity. Such faith works by love; it is not a dead but a living, active, and joyous trust in Jesus. It shows itself in acts of obedience, in a cheerful submission to his ordinances, and in a complete willingness to confess him before men and to obey him in all things. A dead faith is not faith; an inoperative faith is a contradiction in terms. What is it to be a Christian? To obey Jesus Christ with the whole heart. If you have this spirit of obedience you do not lack true faith; you show that you have been born of God, that you are a partaker of the divine nature, and that you are an heir of everlasting life and glory.

Another characteristic of a true Christian is that he does not live in sin—"Whosoever is born of God doth not commit sin" (1 John 3:9). This is a striking passage of Scripture. It is one which has occasioned no small amount of controversy. Both regarding this verse and the sixth of this same chapter there have been many differences of opinion; and doubtless such differences of opinion will continue in the future of the church. Does this statement teach the doctrine of Christian perfection? Does it affirm that the believer is a man sinless in act and thought? So some excellent Christian men and women have said; but does the apostle so teach? There are insuperable objections to this interpretation of his words. If this passage teaches the doctrine of Christian perfection, then it teaches that all Christians are perfect. There is no limitation in this form of statement to one class of Christians rather than another. The word "whosoever" must include all believers of every grade of attainment in the Christian life, and we must affirm of all that they do not and cannot commit sin. But the question arises at once, is this statement true? And the denial must immediately follow the question. No man can affirm that such distinguished examples of faith in God as Abraham, Isaac, and Jacob were sinless. No man dares say with the Scripture history before him that Moses, Job, and Daniel were sinless. No man can truthfully affirm that Peter, John, and Paul were absolutely perfect, even when they reached their highest Christian attainment. Nothing is more certain than that they did not themselves so believe; nothing is more certain than that the word of God does not so affirm regarding these eminent saints. Are we then to suppose that they were not believers? But if all believers are perfect, and these distinguished saints were not perfect, then we are driven to the conclusion that they were not believers. This is surely a painful conclusion, but it is one to which we are inevitably driven if we adopt the idea that this scripture teaches the doctrine of absolute perfection.

But I do not believe that this scripture so teaches. Such an interpretation is not a fair exposition of the passage. The writer uses language which any of us writing in our day might employ, when we simply wish to say of a friend or neighbor that he does not commit or practise willful, habitual, and conscious sin. This thought finds constant expression in the Bible when its writers wish to set forth the idea that a man is truly serving God, and is determinedly avoiding known sin. The Apostle John makes the affirmation very strong, but not stronger than an earnest believer of the doctrine now stated might make it. The passage surely teaches solemn and blessed truths regarding every true believer in Jesus Christ. It certainly sets forth the idea that one who is born of God will not commit habitual sin, will not deliberately sin against his own soul, his neighbor, and his God. The man who intentionally, deliberately, and repeatedly so sins declares that he is a child of Satan rather than a son of God. A true believer may indeed momentarily, under the influence of strong passion, provocation, or temptation, yield to sin; but such a man cannot continuously commit sin and retain the hope that he is a regenerate soul. The noblest Christians see much corruption in their own hearts, and over it they constantly mourn. They will not indeed sin willingly; they will not sin finally. They are restrained by the grace of God in their hearts, so that they shall not wholly fall, so that they shall not finally perish. A true Christian may wander far, but he certainly will penitently return. He will not make sin his normal condition; he will not walk in it and give himself up to its power; he will not be its slave. Sin may be in him, but he will not long be in it. If you know that you hate sin and desire to master it, that you constantly strive against its presence and power, that you desire to gain the victory over every form of evil, rest assured that you are born from above, and that you are truly a child of God. Evil thoughts may sweep through the soul, but if you do not welcome their approach and cherish their presence, you are not their slave. Quaintly has it been said: " I cannot help having the birds fly over my head, but if I have the use of my hands, I can prevent them from making nests in my hair." So if you give evil thoughts no welcome, no quarter, you need not let them rob you of your Christian hope and the joy of divine sonship. But guard, oh, prayerfully guard, your soul in the light of this scripture against indulging in known sin against God.

A true Christian doeth righteousness—"Every one that doeth righteousness is born of him" (1 John 2 : 29). This verse stands in close relations to an interesting train of reasoning. The thought is that all who have a true knowledge of God know that he is righteous; and the apostle means to say that any one who claims to be born of God must be, at least in his purpose and endeavor, righteous also. No man may claim this relationship except he bear this character. It is told that Alexander the Great said to a cowardly soldier, who bore his own name, "You must either change your character or your name." So every man who bears the name of Jesus Christ must possess a Christly character, or he ought immediately to drop the Christly name. This important truth deserves to be constantly emphasized; it is a truth worthy of all acceptation. Christ stands out conspicuously before the church and the world as the righteous One. The man who claims to be born of God must possess the character belonging to the true children of God's family. Righteousness is both imputed and imparted. We have no reason to believe that we have received the forgiving grace of God in our souls except we live the life of God in our relations with men. It is a severe criticism to make of a man, who professes to be a Christian, that he is very pious godward, but very "shaky" manward. The true believer doeth righteousness, not to win the favor of God, not to merit salvation; but, having received salvation as God's free gift, he doeth righteousness from the promptings of love and gratitude. No man can be saved simply by his good works; but no man can be saved without good works. We have no proof of inward life in God except by outward acts of Christian service. As a matter of fact, if we are dishonest, unjust, untruthful in our relations with men, we have no evidence for ourselves, and can give no evidence to others, that we are the children of God. We may at times be exalted to the third heavens with seraphic visions and ecstatic raptures, but if we are impure in life, untruthful in speech, and unholy in act, our raptures and visions are worse than worthless. Our rightness of life will show God's righteousness in us by faith. If, as the fruit of our faith in Christ, we are living rightly toward our neighbors, our families, ourselves, and our God, we may rest assured that we are born of God.

A true Christian will love his brethren—"Every one that loveth is born of God" (1 John 4 : 7). A glance at the context shows that this verse introduces a new topic of discussion, which continues to the end of the chapter. We all know that the Apostle John was the apostle of love, and that this heavenly topic was his chosen theme. All his natural instincts, as well as his special relations to his Lord, peculiarly fitted him for the discussion of this heavenly theme. In the earlier part of this chapter he concluded what he wished to say concerning the trying of spirits, and with this verse he returns to his former exhortation to brotherly love. Men of the world love and seek their own; so Christians should love and seek the things of the new life and love. There is a law of moral gravitation in the Christian life and character, as truly as of physical gravitation in the physical universe. Love is of God. He is its blessed fountain. Christians show that they love him whom they have not seen by loving their brethren whom they see. From the lips of Jesus John learned the truth taught in this verse when Christ said, "A new commandment give I unto you, that ye love one another." John never forgot the time when he pillowed his head on the bosom of his divine and loving Lord; and years after he learned the lesson. He echoed the truth when he said, "We know that we have passed from death unto life because we love the brethren." A man who is born of God must love those who also have been born of God. Differences in social conditions, in intellectual attainments, and in spiritual acquirements, will exist among true Christians; but they will love one another fervently, notwithstanding these differences. They may not love all equally. Christ did not.

He loved Peter, James, and John with a special affection; he loved Mary and Martha and their brother Lazarus with a peculiar tenderness. We also shall have our preferences, but no true believer can hate his brother. We must, of course, understand that the love here spoken of is love toward God, and love to men of which God is the author. The term is limited necessarily to the subject under discussion; it cannot mean every kind of love, whatever may be its source or object. There may be love to one's wife, children, and friends, whose existence would not prove necessarily that he who cherishes it is a true believer. There may be much benevolence toward the poor and much consideration toward all men on the part of many who are not thereby true believers. The love here spoken of is love to God, love to Jesus Christ, love to the children and cause of God, and not love in a general and promiscuous sense. Do you possess and manifest this heavenly love? Can you say at this moment, in the presence of God, that with all your conscious weakness and sinfulness you do earnestly and sincerely love him? Do you know that you love the society and companionship of Christians? Can you affirm that by the tests which you apply to your love for parents, for wife, for children, you love the Lord Jesus Christ? Then know without doubt or fear that you are truly a child of God and a candidate for heaven. If we love God aright there is no other place but heaven to which God could send us. Oh, seek and possess this heavenly love now, and then rejoice in the assurance which it gives that its possessors are born of God.

A true Christian keeps himself and Satan touches him not—"He that is begotten of God keepeth himself, and that wicked one toucheth him not" (1 John 5 : 18). This is a remarkable affirmation. We, of course, understand that no man can keep himself by his own power. If men could so keep themselves there would be no appropriateness in the prayer of Christ, that God should keep them from the evil. God alone is the keeper of his saints; only he whom God keeps is truly kept. We are expressly taught that we are kept by the power of God through faith unto salvation. If there is a mansion and crown reserved in heaven for us, we are preserved for that crown and mansion. A Christian will use all his endeavors to keep himself from sin, and by God's grace he will finally win the victory. It is most inspiring to know that the wicked one toucheth not the true believer. Did not Satan touch Christ? Are we not conscious that he now touches us? The statement means that Christ has so repelled all his assaults that he cannot really harm the weakest of God's true saints; that he cannot wound the believer to the heart; and that he cannot destroy the divine principle of life in the soul. Satan may indeed tempt, sift, buffet, and grieve a true Christian, but he cannot finally overcome or destroy him. Blessed be Christ, he overcame sin both for himself and for us! The believer is yet to bruise Satan under his heel. If the old serpent wounded the heel of the promised deliverer, he had to put his head under the deliverer's heel in order to inflict the wound. Satan assumed a terrible risk when he put his head under the heel of the Lord's Christ. There are some Christians who live constantly on the mountain tops of faith and in the unclouded sunshine of God's presence. Satan cannot disturb their peace, cannot dampen their joy, or lessen their comfort. They can turn against him the shield of faith, so that he cannot wound them with his darts. They can each say as did Christ, "Get thee behind me, Satan." Blessed be the Lord Jesus, who said to his chosen people, "I give unto them eternal life, and they shall never perish, neither shall any [man or devil] pluck them out of my hand." The train of thought here is climacteric. No one is specified. The word man in our common version is added; the original is unspeakably strong. The Lord said that no one, man, devil, or any creature whatsoever, should be able to pluck his children out of his hand; and in the next verse it is affirmed that no one shall be able to pluck them out of his Father's hand. The idea is that as they lie safely and lovingly in Christ's hand, the Father places his hand over that of Jesus, and between the hands of Father and Son believers are absolutely and eternally safe. Here the doctrine of the preservation of the saints is emphatically and sublimely taught. Should a true believer ever perish, the declaration of Christ would be falsified and the honor of God imperiled.

A true Christian gains the victory over the world—"For whosoever is born of God overcometh the world" (1 John 5 : 4). I love the victorious side of the Christian life. Such a passage as this is to me stirring as martial music. This passage is a glorious climax to the progress of our thought in developing the evidences of conversion. If we overcome this world we have also overcome the god of this world. Our course of thought has led up to the crown and the throne. Such exaltation is the Christian's privilege and glory. The world is not a friend of Christ's; its precepts and principles, its maxims and morals, are often opposed to Jesus Christ. There is a conflict between the Christian and the world, and we are here taught that the true Christian has secured the victory. John repeats for us the words of Jesus, "In the world ye shall have tribulation, but be of good cheer, I have overcome the world." We may not expect to escape the tribulations, but we may hope to win the victory. The white-robed throng seen in apocalyptic vision by this same John "came out of great tribulation." But they overcame through the blood of the Lamb. Because Christ overcame the world we may also be victorious. We are to regard the world as a vanquished foe, for "greater is he that is in us, than he that is in the world." We are to be in the world, but not of it. It has been well said that a ship is not in danger because it is in the water; it is in danger only when the water comes freely into it. Our danger is not in our being in the world, but only when the world comes into us.

Can we claim in the light of this last test to be Christians? Are we truly overcoming the world? Does it lie vanquished at our feet? If so, our victory is transcendently glorious. Let us then endure as seeing him who is invisible. This sight of the invisible God is a mighty inspiration in the struggle of life. Faith in the invisible enables us to do the impossible. Only such faith can overcome the world. Such faith made Abraham, Moses, and Joshua triumphant amid every form of opposition. Such faith gave us the Latimers and Ridleys, the Luthers and Calvins, the Bunyans and Baxters, the Whitefields and Wesleys, and the Judsons and Careys, the Spurgeons and Moodys, and such faith to-day is upholding millions of God's saints who are bearing the burdens and sorrows of life, and who amid the shouts of angels and of just men made perfect will receive their reward. Oh, for such faith to-day, faith which overcomes the world, which destroys death, which vanquishes hell, and which utterly defeats Satan; a faith which comes from the home and heart of God, and which leads its possessor up to that home and heart as an eternal dwelling-place.

XII

THE TESTED DISCIPLESHIP

"Then said Jesus unto his disciples, if any man will come after me, let him deny himself, and take up his cross, and follow me." Matt. 16 : 24.

XII

WITH the twenty-first verse of this chapter, our Lord begins a new epoch in his earthly life; this new feature of his mission antedated his crucifixion about nine months. Up to this time he had spoken but little to his disciples regarding his approaching death, and when he spoke of that event, the allusion was made in vague terms rather than in plain and definite statements. Our Lord was a wise teacher; he gave instruction to his disciples only as they were able to receive it. He himself told them at the close of his life that he had many things to say unto them, but they were not able even then to bear them; and they certainly were not able early in his ministry to bear full, free, and definite statements regarding the death which he was to suffer on the ignominious cross. All their thoughts of the Messiah were thoughts of triumph and glory, thoughts of national honor and of universal fame. All their thoughts of the cross were associated with darkness, gloom, excruciating agony, and unspeakable shame. It was not a Jewish but a Roman method of punishment, and the idea that the Messiah of ancient hope and of national glory should die upon the cross was utterly unthinkable by a patriotic and devout Jew. Can it be that the long-expected Messiah, who is to rule the world, is to die a shameful death? Such a thought is too astounding to be believed or even conceived. Our Lord, therefore, did not fully reveal the facts regarding that death until the close of his ministry.

In the verses which immediately precede the text, we see that he made a partial revelation of himself as the Messiah, and he received from the apostles, with Peter as their spokesman, a frank avowal of their faith in him as the Christ, the Son of the living God. That avowal encouraged him to make himself known to them more fully than ever before. He wished them to understand what was before him and them; but they were like men stunned by what was to them a dreadful and incredible disclosure. The Apostle Peter is startled by the statement made by his Lord. No doubt this disciple was somewhat flattered by the commendation that Christ had given him, and he now assumed a position of superiority toward the Lord Jesus. He now acts the part of an older brother, or of a confidential friend; perhaps the part of a trusted inferior who presumes to expostulate with his superior. Peter could not bear the thought that his Lord should suffer and die, so he seems to have drawn him aside to make a personal remonstrance, and to rebuke him, virtually saying: "God be gracious unto thee; be it far from thee, Lord; this thing shall not be unto thee." He had probably been so elated by the honors given him by Christ, that his ardor and self-confidence led him to attempt thus to control his Lord's conduct.

Jesus saw that all the disciples were unfavorably impressed by this patronizing familiarity on the part of Peter; and so, with keen sensitiveness, he quickly turns and gives Peter a cutting rebuke. Just before Peter had been spoken of as the rock; now the rock becomes a stone of stumbling; it becomes an offense to the Lord. We are reminded of the language that our Lord used toward Satan, in the fourth chapter and the tenth verse of this Gospel, when he said, "Get thee hence, Satan"; so when Peter tempted him, he said, using the same language of repulsion and abhorrence, "Get thee behind me, Satan." It was a terrible rebuke to be called Satan. It is a wonder that Peter did not shrink before such a rebuke. The believing confessor is suddenly changed into a presumptuous rebuker; and he is, in turn, rebuked by the Lord whom he had confessed. I wonder that those who put Peter above all the disciples, are not impressed by the thought that he alone of all the disciples was called by Christ "Satan." He was acting the part of Satan in coming between Jesus and the cross; and there are many men to-day acting the part of Peter. They practically deny that Christ ever went to the cross as a sacrifice for men; they are willing to honor him as a loving Saviour, and as the ideal man; but they deny him as the atoning sacrifice. It seems to me that to each one of such preachers and laymen Christ might turn and say, as he did to Peter: "Get thee behind me, Satan; thou art an offense unto me; for thou savorest not of the things that be of God, but those that be of men." Peter would have Christ merely a worldly Messiah. So men still judge regarding his cross of shame. Oh, blessed truth! The crown of thorns was a crown of glory; the reed, given in mockery, was a sceptre of immeasurable dominion. So now, standing beside Christ and his disciples, listening to the rebuke given him by Peter, and to his rebuke given in turn to Peter, we see that his private remonstrance with Peter led to the public declaration before the people, as we learn from Mark, of the conditions of discipleship. We are extremely fortunate in having these conditions given in Christ's own words. It was the prerogative of Jesus Christ, as King of Zion, to state the conditions on which men may enter into that kingdom. Nothing is more impressive in the Gospels than the absolute honesty of the Master. He would never inveigle a man into his kingdom by letting down its high standard of admission.

If you look at the text you will discover that it gives us four conditions of discipleship, complying with which, and only by complying with which, can we be Christ's disciples. The first condition *is a willingness to enter Christ's service* —" If any man will." Bear in mind that the word " will " is not the future tense of the verb to be, but it is an entirely different word. It might be translated, " if any man is willing," or " desires " to come after me. We have, then, as the first condition, clearly implied, if not formally stated, that a man must willingly enter the service of the Lord Jesus. Christ will not force men, except by the drawing of his love, to enter into that kingdom. There must be a deliberate choice. The young man who ran toward Christ was rich, was earnest, was enthusiastic, and was beautiful in many elements of character. Christ laid down the conditions to him, and this young man was not willing to comply. But Christ did not make the standard lower to accommodate that rich young man. Millionaires certainly were rare among the followers of Christ. Could not Christ lower the standard a little to have a man who could pay all the bills? To secure a man who could write his check for a large amount? A man who could command the respect and influence the conduct of wealthy business men? No doubt Christ would have been glad to have such a man; but to win even him Christ would not lower the standard. Christ will not exalt the standard in order to shut out a poor fisherman; it remains the same for the rich young man and the poor fisherman.

In the very nature of the case, men cannot be forced by physical authority into the service of the Lord Jesus. Involuntary obedience is not obedience. The man who cannot but obey does not really obey. We must be free to choose, else we are not responsible for the choice we make. If men are not free to choose they are machines; the idea that they are not free to choose throws the responsibility of their eternal perdition upon God. Such hyper-Calvinism is a welcome doctrine in hades. I would relieve God from such responsibility and throw it upon you. You are free to choose, and you know it; you are free to reject, and you must assume the exalted but terrible responsibility of making a choice. If this element of free-will be not recognized, then there is no good on the one side and no bad on the other. God made Adam free. He had every inducement to obey God; but in the exercise of his freedom, without which he would not have been man, he disobeyed God. Suppose God had made him physically unable to take the fruit; he would then outwardly have obeyed God. But if he had desired to take it he would still spiritually have disobeyed God. There would have been no merit in his refusal to take it if it had been physically impossible for him to eat thereof. All the deliverances of our own consciousness, and all the commandments of the inspired word, teach us that we are free, and that God is a sovereign. Reconcile these two truths we cannot, believe them we must. Here then are the conditions. Comply with them and you are saved, refuse and you are lost, and the responsibility of that loss is your own. The bitterest drop in the cup of remorse is that each man throughout eternity must say, "I alone am to blame. God put before me life, and I took death; God put before me Christ, and I chose Satan; God put before me heaven, and I chose hell." Oh, the bitter pangs of remorse when men are conscious of their own sins in this regard!

God is dogmatic; but God is never reasonless, never arbitrary, never capricious. God always is and must be a dogmatist. God never hesitates; should he hesitate he would cease to be God. Did you ever notice that Christ never said, "I think so," "I trust so," "I hope so"? Profoundly impressed were those who heard Christ with the idea that "he taught as one having authority, and not as the scribes." Christ was never in doubt. He spoke instantly, he spoke decisively, he spoke affirmatively, he spoke authoritatively. Christ does not quote authorities as did the scribes. They quoted other scribes. They and the Pharisees quoted laws and traditions; he did not speak merely as an authoritative expounder of the law, but as himself the divine Lawgiver and final Judge. Christ spoke of the other world as if he were as familiar with it as with this world; he spoke of God as familiarly as your son speaks of you, his father. Christ was dogmatic. Marvelous was his conception of his authority as expressed in his "I say unto you." The last word is spoken when Jesus speaks. Not so when any earthly philosopher speaks; not so when Bacon spoke; not so when the scientists of our day, dogmatic as some are, speak. They quote other authorities. Here stands a Galilean peasant as Lord of all worlds and King in every realm. He never hesitates; he never doubts; he never questions. O blessed, O divine dogmatist. Jesus was God, or he was not a good man; he was God, or he was a hopeless lunatic; he was God, or he was an unpardonable egotist. There is no logical middle ground between these extremes. I love to feel the authority in the words of the Lord Jesus Christ. I repeat, if God would hesitate he would cease to be God. He is always dogmatic. Here is one condition, "if any man is willing." Are you willing? Will you enter now? Will you take Christ just now, and just as you are? Will you march with me now to the music of Christ's name, and be inspired by the glory of Christ's presence?

The second condition is *the renunciation of self and all selfish interests*—"let him deny himself." Christ's hearers were to learn what was required of them ; they were to renounce self and follow their Lord. Such a renunciation was sometimes known by the Gentile proselyte as "the new birth," and the Jews used such language when any person came out of heathenism into Judaism. But Christ gave it a nobler meaning. Peter wished Christ to spare himself, but Christ virtually said, "I cannot spare myself. No man can spare himself if he is to serve God and his fellow-men." Christ said, "He that loveth his life shall lose it; but he that loseth his life for my sake, shall find it." No man can serve himself and serve Christ ; no man can be a self-seeker and be a true follower of the Lord Jesus. There is a self-love which is right, but the moment that it passes over into selfishness it is wrong. Selfishness in Cain makes him ask, "Am I my brother's keeper?" Selfishness in Satan led him to exalt himself above all that is called God. Christ had no self-life ; from his cradle to his cross he lived for others. His life was a continual death ; he died daily that he might live divinely. We must die daily if we are to live Christly lives. Would to God that our self-life were crucified with Christ upon the cross ! Would that the Christ-life might be in every act, in every word, and in every thought ! This self-crucifixion is one of the great, indispensable, fundamental laws of all noble beings; the servant cannot be above his master. This element is not characteristic of the Christian life alone, but it is a fundamental element in every truly noble life. If Wendell Phillips is to be the leader of the hosts of liberty he must die to self, to ambition, to honor, as he did die on the afternoon of October 21, 1835, when he left his office on Court Street, Boston, and going out saw the crowd on Washington Street, and in the midst of the mob Garrison, bare-headed and bedraggled, but with head erect, face calm, and eyes flashing, and with a rope around his waist, as he is dragged toward the City Hall, while the mob is shouting for his life—then Phillips devoted himself to the destruction of American slavery.

We must die as did Wilberforce, when he dedicated himself to God and to the abolition of the slave trade in England's colonies. Every man must die to self if he is to live to God and to men. Every college student must die to indolence, to indulgence, and to laziness, if he is to live for study, for triumph, for honor. Every business man must die to lower things if he is to live for higher things in his business. The same law applies to the Christian life; we are to die to our lower self that we may live to our nobler self, that we may live for Jesus Christ. We are to renounce our sinfulness. You all know that every tree has a great tap-root, and that in proportion as the tap-root strikes down into God's deep earth the trunk shoots into God's sunshine. Cut off many of the branches and rootlets of the tree and it will still grow; but cut off the tap-root and you destroy the tree, for it stands in such close relations to the trunk. So self is the tap-root of the Judas tree in life, and until that tap-root is cut off by the grace of God, the Judas tree will bring forth its deadly fruit. Oh, may God help you to cut off the tap-root of sin and make you live for him and for all about you! Love for even little sins, as men judge, will destroy the noblest ideals of life. In the Civil War a Federal warship had what was thought to be only a trifling, superficial leak; and although observed, it was not deemed necessary to countermand the order that she was to take part in the battle. The fight began; this ship was in the midst of the conflict. The crisis of the battle had come; and it was then found that through this leak the sea water had oozed into the powder magazine. On that leak turned the fortunes of the day, and the battle was lost. There really are no little sins; only as sin is confessed and forgiven is its terrible danger removed.

A little flaw in a ruby prevented England from buying it at a fabulous price; the crown jeweler discovered the fracture and the value was reduced by thousands of pounds, and the ruby was rejected from the regalia of Great Britain. We are told that Canova, when about to begin his statue of the great Napoleon, having carefully examined a splendid block of marble which had been secured at great cost, discovered a tiny red line running through its upper portion, and he refused to put his chisel further upon it. That red line vitiated the block. So God, the great Sculptor, in carving out the statue of an ideal man must reject every stain caused by sin. A slight streak of selfishness in a man's life will color all his acts, all his words, all his thoughts. O men, I would have you to-day kings and priests unto God. O women, I would have you princesses and queens unto God. I would have you nail it to the tree; I would have you bury it in Joseph's tomb. Then I would see in the glad Easter morning of your spiritual life a personal faith and a Christly love as you walk forth in newness of life.

And now let us hurriedly glance at the third condition: it is *a willingness to bear the cross*— "and take up his cross." The Jews, as Doctor Broadus, in commenting on the text, has shown, were familiar with the punishment of crucifixion. It was long common in Italy, in Egypt, and in Western Asia. At least one hundred years previous to the time of our Lord, King

Alexander Janneus crucified eight hundred rebels at Jerusalem. It is also said that under Antiochus Epiphanes many Jews were crucified, and that two thousand were crucified during the proconsulate of Varus, because of a revolt which followed the death of Herod the Great. It was customary that a condemned person should carry his cross to the place of execution. The disciples could not, therefore, misunderstand our Lord's allusion; they understood that he was like one who was marching to crucifixion. They would learn also that they likewise must be ready for suffering and death. Not only could he not avoid the cross, but they also must bear it if they are to be his disciples.

Now, I am not going to fall into the error into which many Christians fall, when they represent the Christian life as only a cross-bearing, crying, sighing life. The word of God represents the Christian life as a life of triumph and of glory; a life whose symbol is the upsoaring eagle; a life that runs without weariness; a life that walks without faintness. Men speak of a life of sin as a life of pleasure, but so to speak is a mistake; it is a life of slavery; it is a life to be pitied by men, a life to be pitied and almost despised by angels and God. "Take up his cross." I want you to notice the language here used. I often see many young Christians standing beside the cross and looking at it wearily; I see other young Christians taking hold of one end of the cross and dragging it along. But Jesus did not say, "Let him deny himself, and drag his cross." He said, "Let him deny himself, and take up his cross." The cross, when taken up, is by the alchemy of divine grace transformed into a ladder, up which we may climb into the sunshine of God's presence and into the enjoyment of God's love. Sweetly did Rutherford say of Christ's yoke: "It is a burden such as wings are to a bird, or as sails are to a ship." A blessed burden are wings to a bird; a joyous burden are sails to a ship; and such a burden is Christ's yoke to all who put it on.

The cross is the symbol of all the forms of suffering which we have to bear in our Christian life. I would not ask you to go out to find a cross; I would not ask you to bring down crosses on your head and shoulders. But I dare not permit you by any cowardly, unmanly, un-Christian conduct to run away from your cross. A good rule is never to go out of the way to meet a cross, and never to go aside to miss a cross; but just to move on in the Christian life which God in his providence has marked out, taking the crosses which he sees best to send. O beloved, take up your cross, and it will be light. The Christian life was never so much to me as it is now. Jesus was never so precious as now. Jesus, blessed Jesus! Would that now we all would open our hearts to receive him, giving them up to him as his throne!

And this leads me to say just a word about the last condition: *we are to follow Christ.* We are not to go before him, but to follow him. "Follow me"; this is the divine command. Obedience is the proof of love; Christ in his baptism fulfilled all righteousness. Righteousness in the record of that event is thought of as a cup; the cup was held out to Christ, and if he had not been baptized it would not have been full; to fulfill is to fill full." Rightly he said, "Lo, I come to do thy will, O God." Let us do God's will to-day by following Christ. If we do, we shall at last follow him into glory. In paths of duty on earth Christ always precedes his people; in heaven we shall follow the Lamb whithersoever he goeth. I want to see the print of my Saviour's feet, and there I want to put my feet. "Follow me." Yes, but there are great difficulties in the way. Still Christ says, "Follow me." Yes, but there are inconsistent Christians. "Follow thou me." Yes, but there are parts of the Bible which I do not understand. Christ again replies, "Follow me." Enter Christ's school and you will learn the obscure lesson. All who do his will soon come to know his doctrine. That is the eternal law; that is the blessed experience. Follow me to the cross, to the tomb, to the resurrection; follow me up the shining heights of glory; follow me through the gates of pearl and along the streets of gold. Let our glad response be, O Christ, draw us by the cords of thy love, and we will run after thee.

XIII

THE INESTIMABLE POSSESSION

"... Knowing in yourselves that ye have in heaven a better and an enduring substance." Heb. 10 : 34.

XIII

ASSUMING that the Apostle Paul is the author of the Epistle to the Hebrews, we have in the early part of the verse from which the text is taken his acknowledgment of the sympathy of the Hebrew Christians with him when he was a prisoner. We do not know what particular imprisonment is in the mind of the writer. Perhaps it was some occasion when he was a prisoner in Judea, as it is generally believed that those to whom he wrote resided for the most part there. It is certain that the Hebrew Christians at the time this Epistle was written were suffering persecution. Efforts were making to induce them to apostatize from the Christian faith. The author designs, therefore, to show that all that was truly great in Judaism was found in Christianity. It is certain that these early disciples suffered much because of their loyalty to the Christian faith. Over against the great sacrifices spoken of in the early part of the verse, the writer places the compensations which these Hebrew Christians possessed and enjoyed. This leads us to speak of the inestimable possession which their Christian faith secured; and the characteristics of this possession are finely suggested for us in the text. Let us specify these characteristics that we may rejoice in the blessings bestowed upon Christian believers in that early day, and enjoyed by Christian believers in our day.

1. It is a *known* possession — "knowing in yourselves." It is the privilege and duty of Christian men to know that they belong to God. It is unfortunate that many persons suppose that they manifest a commendable humility when they express doubt as to their acceptance of Christ and their possession of Christian faith. We are not to suppose that reference is here made to any internal and occult knowledge of our relationship with Christ. The reference is rather to the assurance that all true believers may have that they have laid up for themselves in heaven a better inheritance than earth can ever bestow. The hesitancy regarding this knowledge may sometimes be due to personal peculiarities. There are those who are timid, hesitant, and unassertive in all their relations in life. Christianity does not destroy individual peculiarities. Idiosyncrasies remain after the grace of God has truly come into the heart. Divine grace alone did not make David a poet, nor Paul a logician. Divine grace sanctified the poetic genius of the one and the logical acumen of the other. We often misunderstand what is true Christian humility. True humility takes

the place which God offers; true humility accepts the honors which God bestows. True humility will not insist upon calling ourselves slaves when God calls us sons. We make religion obscure, but God intends that all its principles should be simple, readily adopted, and clearly affirmed. We throw a veil of mystery over the act of faith when that act is concerned with religious things; but so far as the act itself is concerned it is not different, as an exercise of our faculties from the act of faith regarding material things. The difference is in the object rather than in the act of faith. It is a thousand pities that we have relegated religious faith to a territory widely removed from acts of faith in human relations. Religion, if we give the word one derivation, is simply a binding back of the soul to God from whom it has been separated; or, if we give it another derivation, it is but the gathering or collecting of our faculties for religious service. In either case it is common sense consecrated to its highest uses.

It is most unfortunate that erroneous teaching has so largely mystified our religious thinking. Often the importance of the subject leads some to doubt the possibility of knowing God and our relations to him. We ought to be absolutely assured that this knowledge is possible. If it were not possible, why should we be exhorted to make our calling and election sure? The experience of many of God's children justifies us in affirming the certainty of this knowledge. Assuredly Job knew that his Redeemer lived; assuredly Paul knew that he had committed all his interests for time and eternity to Jesus Christ; and assuredly the Apostle John knew that he and others had passed from death unto life. It is equally certain that we all may realize that Christ has become our personal Lord and Redeemer. We may as truly know that we love God as that we love mother, wife, or child. This is no peculiar, no unique knowledge. It rests upon evidence as does knowledge concerning our fellow-men. We certainly may know whether we love the word of God, the service of God, the house of God, and the people of God. To say that a man cannot know these things is to impugn his common sense, is to question his sanity, is often to doubt his piety.

This knowledge also is very blessed; many a true believer goes mourning all his days for want of such knowledge. He makes his unjustifiable doubts synonymous with commendable piety. Can God be pleased with us when we doubt his word? Would our fellow-men be pleased with us if we doubt their word? Let us rise to the lofty possibilities of faith and assurance as the children of God, the heirs of God, and the joint-heirs with Jesus Christ.

2. This is a *present* possession—" knowing in

yourselves that ye have." We err greatly in referring all our blessings to the future life. The men and women who believe in Jesus Christ become at once the possessors of inestimable possessions. There is a treasure for each believer here and now. If a man does not permit heaven to enter into him in this life, he will never enter into heaven in the life that is to come. We enter into fellowship with Jesus Christ and he with us; here and now the heavenly life begins which there and hereafter is to be enlarged and ennobled. The word of God everywhere emphasizes the fact that true believers already have eternal life. Our Lord expressly affirms that "he that heareth my word and believeth on him that sent me hath everlasting life." Again and again he repeats this thought in a variety of forms of expression. We are guilty of unbelief when we hesitate to accept what Jesus Christ thus frequently and graciously bestows. The Apostle John, writing in the evening of his life, thus speaks: "Beloved, now are we the sons of God, and it doth not yet appear what we shall be; but we know that, when he shall appear, we shall be like him; for we shall see him as he is." Here and now we are the sons of God; here and now we are the heirs of glory; here and now we have entered upon the heavenly life. Let us not hesitate to say so. We are infidel to God's precious promises and unworthy of our own high calling when we doubt these blessed truths. Conscious of all our faults and failings, of our wanderings and rebellions, it is still true that we are the sons and daughters of the Lord Almighty. With deep humility and yet with holy boldness let us claim our privileges as the children of God and the heirs of heaven.

3. This is also a *personal* possession. This truth is implied in the more literal rendering of the first clause of the text. Instead of translating the words as in the Common version, " knowing in yourselves," perhaps we ought to render them, "knowing that in yourselves," or "for yourselves." This latter rendering brings out the thought which it is intended to emphasize at this point in this discourse. We are here reminded of the element of personality which is everywhere found in the word of God and which is revealed in our own consciousness in our relations with God. Personality is immortal. The first cry of a child sounds a note which will echo in eternity. On the mount of Transfiguration Moses and Elijah appeared conversing with Jesus. Moses had been dead about fifteen hundred years and Elijah perhaps a thousand, yet Moses was still Moses and Elijah still Elijah. The personality of each remained, notwithstanding the flight of the centuries. This is a sublime and an equally solemn thought. Religion must be a personal possession. No man can be-

lieve and obey and imitate God by proxy. Each man for himself must appear at the judgment seat of Christ and answer for the deeds done in the body, whether they be good or evil. We cannot appear through the person of any representative in our solemn transactions with God. It is a blessed thought that this inestimable possession becomes a part of our personal moral furniture. It is ingrained in our very souls; it, therefore, can never be taken from the child of God. He who has entered into Christ and has permitted Christ to enter into him has become a partaker of the divine nature. No earthly child of an earthly parent is more truly that parent's in flesh and blood than is every believer essentially God's child. No poverty, however deep, can rob us of this heavenly possession; no wealth, however great, can purchase for us this heavenly possession. It is a gift of God's grace through Jesus Christ, God's Son and our Saviour.

4. This is also a *heavenly* possession. This truth is brought out in the text as found in the Common version of the Scriptures. The reference to heaven, it is only fair to say, is omitted in the later versions, or is so inserted as to imply doubt as to its place in the true text. It is not important to the real meaning whether or not we emphasize this characteristic. Our possession is partly in heaven and partly on the earth. There is laid up for us a crown of righteousness

and an inheritance incorruptible and undefiled and that fadeth not away. This inheritance, we are elsewhere taught, is reserved in heaven for us. Heaven is chiefly a state rather than a place. There can be no heaven anywhere to a man who does not love God; there can be nothing but heaven everywhere to a man who does love God. If we could transfer at once all the wretched inhabitants of hades to the mansions of glory in heaven, so long as they remained unchanged in heart the transfer would bring to them additional misery rather than a blessing. It is positive kindness in God to banish from his presence those who hate him. Men who, because of their love of evil, would be wretched in a tender and heavenly prayer meeting, would be vastly more wretched in heaven itself and in the immediate presence of Christ.

But we know also that heaven is a place; this truth our Lord distinctly affirmed. He assured his disciples that he had gone to prepare a place for them. In this blessed abode there are many mansions, even as there will be innumerable inhabitants. While it is true that streets of gold and harps giving forth melodious music in the immediate presence of Christ cannot make heaven to wicked men, it is true, on the other hand, that these adornments of heaven, together with the beatific vision of Christ, will add unspeakably to the joy already present in the believer's soul. Let us rejoice in this heavenly inheritance; it is reserved in heaven for us, and we are preserved on earth for it. We need it for the completion of our Christian experience and attainment. We are pressing toward the perfect character of our blessed Lord. His righteousness is both imputed and imparted. Thank God, one day we shall awake in his likeness; we shall see him as he is, and then and only then shall our souls be fully satisfied.

5. This is also a *superior* possession. We are distinctly told in the text that we have in heaven "a better and an enduring substance." With what other possession is the heavenly possession compared? Doubtless with the good things which Christians have upon the earth. These Hebrew Christians had lost much of what the world calls its good things. They took joyfully the providences which robbed them of their earthly possessions. Nowhere does the word of God, when rightly understood, make light of the blessings of this life. It was an evil for these early Christians to be deprived of their inheritances and to be turned out of their homes and to be plundered of their goods. It was an evil for them to be obliged to wander about in sheepskins and goatskins, without home, without friends, without peace. It was a wonderful illustration of their trust in God that, although destitute, afflicted, and tormented, they joyfully ac-

cepted their persecution and endured it without complaint and without apostasy from the faith. They lost the lower and they secured the higher good; they were plundered of earthly possessions, but they received heavenly possessions vastly more valuable. The Spirit of God bore witness with their spirits that they were the children of God; they knew fully that heaven was their portion and Christ their Redeemer. Well might they without sorrow be deprived of earthly good when God bestowed upon them heavenly good, compared with which their earthly possessions were as shadow to substance. This world belongs to Christians as it never can to unbelievers. It is possible for the true child of God to get the best things out of both worlds. The Bible nowhere dishonors the world, except so far as that world belongs to Satan and not to Christ. Christ's hand and not Satan's is on the helm of this universe. There are earthly pleasures that are not sinful; these, true Christians may and ought fully to enjoy. In seeking first the kingdom of God they are in the right attitude to have all other good things added unto them. They who live for themselves alone do not receive the best things even of this life, and they lose entirely the good things of the life to come. While the love of money is the root of all evil, the right use of money may be the source of many blessings. God has made this world beautiful to those who see in it marks of his love, his power, and his wisdom. Those who would banish God from his own world banish also all that is most beautiful in nature and most comforting in providence. While a man's life does not consist in the things which he hath, he may so see God's favor in his earthly possessions that they shall become unspeakably valuable to him as the gifts of his Father in heaven. It is an utter mistake to suppose that unchristian men get more joy out of this world, even if this world were all, than do Christian men. The Christian man sees in all the affairs of life tokens of his Father's presence and blessing. As a child can better understand the voice of his father than can a stranger, so the true Christian may be the most intelligent and appreciative student of nature. Its manifold voices are echoes of the one voice of his Father in heaven. He reads God's beautiful thoughts in the flowers, his brilliant thoughts in the stars, and his majestic thoughts in the mountains. The whole world is the incarnation of his Father's thought of love. The undevout scientist is unscientific. But good as is this world, the true child of God knows that in heaven he has a better possession. It is worth vastly more in itself and in what it imparts. It gives the poorest man more than the fabled wealth of Crœsus or that of the multi-millionaires of to-day. It gives peace which neither the world nor the devil can disturb; it imparts a joy which outlasts time and sense, and at last a triple crown—a crown of righteousness, of life, and of glory.

6. It is a *permanent* possession. This truth is implied in the text when this possession is called " an enduring substance." This element enters largely into the superiority of this possession as compared with the good things of this life. All earthly possessions are most precarious. Solomon was right when he affirmed " vanity of vanities, all is vanity." The thought is trite as true, that nothing on earth abides. One is conscious of the majesty and glory of the pyramids partly because they are so ancient and apparently so stable. Kingdoms have risen and fallen, empires have bloomed and withered, republics " have danced into light, and died into the shade"; but the pyramids have remained. The thought that the Sphinx has from time immemorial gazed in sublime silence out over the desert, gives an indescribable charm to its strange face and impressive attitude. But the pyramids are crumbling to the earth; they are lower to-day than once they were. Nothing on the earth abides. Earthly riches take to themselves wings and fly away, or their possessors are soon to be taken from their riches. War, pestilence, famine, commercial embarrassment, financial stringencies, these are all characteristic

of this earth. Thank God there are possessions that are enduring, possessions that outlive time, possessions that lay hold upon eternity. Thank God there is a house not made with hands, eternal in the heavens. Thank God there is a city which hath foundations, a city whose maker and builder is God. Thank God there is an everlasting kingdom. It is a marvelous thought that there are no graves in heaven; that there none are sick and none are weary, but all are filled with joy that is unspeakable and full of glory.

7. This is also a *genuine* possession. It is a possession of "substance." The mind and the heart long for verities as opposed to vanities; for substance as contrasted with shadow. We grow utterly weary of the emptiness, shallowness, and heartlessness of the best things of earth. This substance, as the word in the original teaches, is property, is reality; it is a genuine and sincere possession. Much that we call valuable on earth is largely fictitious; it is a changeable quantity; it depends upon a great variety of unstable conditions. It is estimated rather than inherent values with which in this life we are familiar, and we have at times a sincere longing for real values as opposed to estimated values. The world itself has learned to distinguish sharply between supposed and absolute valuation. All men long for the perma-

nent and the real as opposed to the evanescent and the fanciful. Here is a value that is not dependent upon interested combinations in Wall Street. This value the most experienced Christian cannot adequately appreciate, and un-Christian men are totally incompetent to give it an accurate appraisement. We are discussing to-day the value to trade, to commerce, and to the honor of the American name of sound money. We have learned to distinguish accurately between real and fiat values. Oh, that men were wise concerning the things of eternity as they are regarding the things of time!

Here and now, O men and women, I offer you the sublimest and divinest possession ever promised to the children of men. No poverty need fail to secure it; no wealth can purchase it. It is above all price, above all earthly estimates, above even angelic knowledge and appreciation. Men are to be judged by the choices which they make; he who chooses baubles and rejects diamonds declares himself unspeakably unwise. He who chooses the evanescent things of time and rejects the unspeakable values of eternity declares himself morally insane. How shall we come into this possession? How shall we become the heirs of God and the inheritors of heaven? To redeem your souls Christ died. Without money and without price he offers you adoption into his family and possession of heavenly treasure. Come just as you are, here and now, and receive this pearl of great price, to win which Christ left heaven, wearily trod the earth, and ignominiously died upon the cross. As his ambassador I offer it to you to-day. Open hand and heart to receive it, and you shall go out of this house " knowing in yourselves that ye have in heaven a better and an enduring substance."

XIV

THE RESCUED DISCIPLE

"And the Lord said, Simon, Simon, behold Satan hath desired to have you, that he might sift you as wheat; but I have prayed for thee that thy faith fail not; and when thou art converted strengthen thy brethren." Luke 22: 31, 32.

XIV

THIS text ought to be studied carefully as it is given in the Revised version, which runs thus: "Simon, Simon, behold, Satan asked to have you, that he might sift you as wheat: but I made supplication for thee, that thy faith fail not; and do thou, when once thou hast turned again, stablish thy brethren." There are few passages in that version which bring out at several points the exact thought of the original more clearly than does this one. Every one at all familiar with the word of God in the original, in reading these two verses in the Revised version will get the full flavor of the original text. This translation brings the reader very near to the lips of the great Teacher, and gives the thought very nearly as he intended it should be received.

If you look at the twenty-fourth verse of this chapter, you will see that there was an unseemly and sinful strife among the disciples as to who should be the greatest. It is supposed by many that this strife gave occasion to the words that I have selected as the text this morning. If we go back and inquire concerning the occasion of the strife, we may accept one of two answers.

It is supposed by some that it arose from the request preferred by the mother of James and John, that one of her sons should sit on Christ's right hand and the other on his left, when he should come into his kingdom. This request, it would seem, caused a strife, more particularly between Peter on the one hand and James and John on the other. Or perhaps the occasion of the strife may be found in what is recorded in the sixteenth and eighteenth verses of this same chapter. The disciples thought Christ spoke of a temporal kingdom, as their minds were full of ideas of earthly glory, and these ideas engendered worldly ambition and unholy strife.

As I have said, the strife was more especially between Peter on the one side and James and John on the other. The younger disciples do not seem to have participated in this ambitious contention. These two sons of Zebedee were favorite disciples of Christ. Peter naturally would be jealous of their position and influence; he would plead his seniority, and the special promise which Christ had made to him, as a reason why he should be supreme rather than they. Christ had distinguished these three disciples by peculiar marks of his favor; and he now teaches them a needed lesson. He refers to himself and says that he is greatest who is humblest. This is our Lord's teaching evermore; this is our Lord's example evermore. Christ seems to say to them, "If you indulge this unholy spirit, the question soon shall not be which shall be greatest among you, but the question shall be whether any of you belong to my kingdom." Christ seems to say to them, "If you indulge that spirit, Satan will soon get you all, and you will belong to the kingdom of darkness rather than to the kingdom of light."

Out then of this strife, caused either by one or the other of the occasions of which I have spoken, comes our text. It is quite possible that Peter was responsible for this contention and hence he is rebuked by name.

I ask you, in the first place, to notice Christ's *solemn warning to Peter*—"Simon, Simon, behold, Satan hath desired to have you." You will observe in this warning that the Apostle Peter is reminded of his natural weakness. It is observable also that this reminder comes partly in the very title which Christ uses in addressing him, "Simon, Simon." That was Peter's old name; that was Peter's unconverted name; that was the name which he had before his call to discipleship. This fact you will observe if you refer to the time when Christ first called Peter. Did you ever stop to think that Peter was the first convert that Christ made during his public ministry? He was Christ's first trophy among those who were to be numbered among his chosen Twelve. He was the first person brought to Christ by one who was to be numbered among the Twelve; and Peter's name at that time was not Peter, but Simon; and Christ's prophetic words to Peter were that his name should be changed, and instead of being Simon, son of Jonas, it should be Peter, the rock. Those words were still prophetic, for Peter was not firm, not stable, not immovable. And you will remember that after Peter had denied his Lord, and was so severely tested, Christ does not call him Peter, but says, "Simon, lovest thou me?" So by the use of this name Christ reminds Peter of his natural weakness, of his old man, of his human frailty. "Simon, Simon, behold, Satan demanded or asked for you." The repetition of the name is a mark of personal love as well as of emphatic warning; it is love shown by the warning. We need often to be reminded in the same way of our old name and of our natural weakness. We profess to belong to Christ; we profess to have surrendered the whole territory of our being to the Lord Jesus; but we are obliged to confess that we often find that parts of the territory are still unsubdued, and so we are exhorted to watch and pray lest we enter into temptation. "Let him that thinketh he standeth take heed lest he fall."

But the warning also reminded Peter of the wiles of his adversary. "Satan asked to have you." I give here the rendering of the new version, because it brings out the true thought, which is not even suggested by the version in common use. There we have "Satan hath desired to have you." That might be simply an unspoken thought, an unuttered desire. But the desire is not unspoken; it is earnestly and verbally voiced. "Satan asked to have you," or, as in the margin, "obtained you by asking," which is a still stronger expression; this is surely a striking and startling fact which is here announced, and it suggests the case of Job. When the sons of God came to present themselves before the Lord, Satan came also; although Satan is a fallen angel, yet he is obliged to come into the presence of Jehovah to report. He charged Job with serving God for gain. God gave Satan leave to test Job up to the point of simply sparing his life. God still maintained control over Satan, practically saying, "Thus far shalt thou go, and no farther." Satan is powerful, but he is not omnipotent; he is wise, but he is not omniscient. His power is limited, and it is also delegated. Now we see from the original of our text, and also from the Revised version, that a somewhat similar transaction took place in the case of Peter. Satan asked that he might have all the disciples. He already had Judas; he nearly got Peter, and he desired all. He charged Job, as we have seen, with serving God for mercenary purposes; and now he brings the same charges against the disciples. He virtually says, "You want to be governors of a vast territory; you want to have great temporal power, and you are willing to serve the Lord for the loaves and fishes of worldly good." The real meaning of the word Satan is a deceiver, an adversary, and the word devil means an accuser, a slanderer. Satan slanders God to men, and men to God. He is represented in the book of Revelation as the "accuser of our brethren." And no doubt he is accusing you and me to Christ this morning, and is also misrepresenting Christ to us. We all need all the power of Christ to deliver us from Satan's wiles.

But, furthermore, Christ's warning to Peter illustrated the kind of temptation to which he was exposed. Peter stood then on the border of a great temptation and a great fall, and Christ saw his danger and solemnly and lovingly warned him. Satan's prayer was that he might sift the disciples as wheat. Now, we know that sifting is a cleansing and purifying process; it separates the chaff from the wheat. But I cannot think that Satan desired to remove the chaff and retain the wheat. There are two meanings to this part of Satan's prayer: He might have simply desired to bring the chaff to view, to prove if possible that there was no wheat and that all was chaff. Or another meaning is the more likely: It is that Satan desired now to annoy the disciples, to disturb Christ, and in the end to secure the utter apostasy of the disciples.

There was much in Peter that ought to be removed. There was much in Peter which perhaps we may not call positive sin, but which was an element of weakness. Peter was too bulky and needed to be reduced in size. In spiritual life "the half is often far more than the whole." As John Bunyan quaintly says: "Peter needed to be very much tumbled up and down." The "old man" was here brought into remembrance. This reminder, perhaps, was helpful to Peter; it is helpful, occasionally at least, to us all. There is much in the process of growth that is not necessary after the growth has been secured. We use the word "chaff" as the synonym of what is worthless, but if you will look at the growing wheat you will see proofs of the divine wisdom in the protection of the grain by the chaff. We ought not to despair when we find young Christians sometimes quite too much elated with pride, when we find them too bulky with chaff. There is a good deal of chaff in the best of men, but the Lord Jesus will blow it away with the wind of some sort of trial. I can name men who thirty or forty years ago were considered harsh and severe, bulky and inflated, who now are known to be sweet and mellow, soft and beautiful, reduced and humble.

Doubtless Christ intended to overrule Satan's temptation of Peter, so that the chaff of Peter's life should disappear and so that the pure wheat should remain. We may be sure that this result was partly secured. He probably was the oldest of all the disciples; he probably was chiefly responsible for the strife. He must, therefore, personally receive his Lord's rebuke. May we all learn the lessons Christ would teach us in all the trials of our lives.

Notice, in the second place, *Christ's great encouragement to Peter*—" But I made supplication for thee, that thy faith fail not." This is the more correct rendering. Oh, how comforting it is to know that Christ makes supplication for us. Christ's prayers are a strong wall about his people. In that wonderful chapter of John, the true Lord's Prayer, the seventeenth, we have an illustration of Christ's intercessory prayer on behalf of his people. He prayed not only for the disciples who had witnessed his temptations, but for all who should believe on him through their word, and this petition included all true believers to-day.

I want you to observe that this is a personal prayer. There is a change in the pronoun between the early and latter part of the text. This personal and discriminating element in Christ's prayer and sympathy is tender and beautiful in his relations to his tempted and suffering ones. He comes into close personal relations with each one of us. You think that your circumstances and relations in life are peculiar, that no one was ever tried as you are, that no cross was ever so heavy as yours. Christ comes to you and says: "I know it all, I understand your case perfectly, and I have prayed for thee." It is beautiful to see how Christ came into contact with individuals all through his ministry. I could dwell long on this feature of his work and sympathy. I have often alluded to it. It is to me a very precious thought. For each bruised heart he has a special balm; for every burdened life he has special strength; to every tempted soul he gives peculiar deliverance. This truth is delightfully brought out in the text. Satan asked for "you," you all. The word in the original is in the plural; it included all the disciples as well as Peter. Then we read: "I have prayed for thee." The pronoun is now in the singular; a suggestive contrast surely this is between "you" and "thee." The self-reliant Peter especially needed the prayer of Christ, and Christ prayed for him then, as if Peter alone in the world needed special prayer. This is wonderful love and divine condescension. Was this special prayer for Peter because Peter was so sweet and beautiful in his character? Was it because Peter was more equable in his disposition, more loving in his nature, more charitable in his judgments? Far from it. Peter was often egotistical, self-reliant, boastful, uncharitable, dogmatic. Was not the prayer chiefly because of his weakness, because of his inconstancy, because of his liability to fall? Was not his very weakness a plea to the heart of the almightiness of Jesus Christ? Was not the painful future that was opening before Peter a reason for Christ's prayer?

Our Lord also asks for a particular grace. He does not pray that Satan's power might be destroyed; he does not pray that the thorn should not enter Peter's flesh; he does not pray that he may not be tossed on the sieve. But he prays that his faith may not utterly fail; that he may not fall into Satan's possession and power. We have often been reminded that there are two ways by which we may be helped to carry our burdens. One is to make the burden lighter and the other is to give us more strength. Christ seems to say: "No, no, Peter, Satan must sift you; but I have prayed that thy faith fail not entirely." Faith is the shield that will ward off the fiery darts of Satan. If faith stands, the man will stand. It is easy to exercise faith in Jesus when the air is sweet, when it is perfumed with the breath of praise and prayer, when joy and peace reign in the home, and the sympathy of brethren is manifested in the church; it is easy when it is the rare month of June in heart, home, and church. But when December comes, and the winds are bleak and "flecked with snow," and we are chilled to the bone; when business is bad and friends fail us, oh, then it is hard to have faith. Now Christ prayed, as being the most important grace of all, that Peter's faith fail not. What kind of faith? Faith in God, faith in purity, faith in love, faith in truth, in virtue, in honesty, in character, and right—in a word, faith in God and in ourselves as his children, as the objects of his care and the heirs of his glory. We may be standing to-day on the border of a great temptation. O Christ, thou Son of God and Son of man, pray for us this morning. Keep us by thy grace. Bring us off more than conquerors.

There is just one other thought in connection with that prayer, and I have time now only to touch upon it—Christ's prayer was prevailing prayer. It is as if Christ had said, "Satan is praying and I am praying; there is a contest here, Peter, for your soul." Peter's soul was in the public mart; it was in danger of being secured by Satan, but the Lord Jesus prays. It is a great comfort sometimes to know that the church is praying for us. For years in my ministry I was greatly helped by the knowledge that my mother prayed for me daily. I knew every Sunday when I entered this pulpit that her prayers were ascending to God. And when she went home I was conscious of a great loss, conscious that an element of power must henceforth be wanting in my life. At times there is a great hunger in my heart for her love and in my life for her prayers. But when I know that Christ, who himself said of his prayers to the Father, "I know that thou hearest me always," when I know that he prays for me, neither life nor death can have power to terrify me. It is certain that although there may be failings in a believer's faith there shall not be failure of the believer's faith. Although his faith may be sadly shaken it shall not utterly fall. If left to themselves Christians would certainly fail, but they are kept by the power of God through faith unto salvation.

Peter's case is no exception to this universal and blessed law. He was badly weakened, but he did not entirely fall. The prayer offered by Christ on his behalf was literally answered. Until I discovered from a recent study in the original the exact meaning of the word translated "fail," I was troubled by the apparent contradiction between the prayer of Christ and the conduct of Peter. It once seemed to me as if the prayer had not been answered; it seemed as if Peter's faith did fail. But the more careful study recently given shows the perfect harmony there is between the prayer and the fulfillment. The word translated "fail" is a very strong word. It is the ordinary word fail with a preposition added which gives it the meaning of failing utterly, entirely, completely. This added meaning fully explains the whole case. Peter's faith did partially fail, but it did not fail utterly; he fell, but he did not fall off, did not apostatize, did not forsake his Master fully and finally as did Judas. It is interesting to observe that the word here translated "fail" is used in classic Greek of the eclipse of the sun. We may say that Peter's faith was for the time under an eclipse, but though eclipsed it was not extinguished. Christ's prayer did prevail. Blessed are they for whom he is the Advocate; blessed are they who are included in his prevalent intercession. Let all who listen to my voice now beseech Jesus Christ to become their Advocate with the Father.

And now, very briefly, the last thought, *Christ's practical command to Peter*—"When once thou hast turned again, stablish thy brethren." When a Christian man has wandered from God, he must return to God, or he cannot be either happy or useful. You can never return to the Christian path, after wandering, where you ought to be had you continued on it. You must go back again and do your first works if you have left your first love. He who goes away from God must go back to God. The technical ideas associated with the word "converted" obscure the true thought here. It is simply turned, turned back from wandering, restored to duty after wandering in folly and sin. Oh, that all who have wandered would to-day go back to God. Am I speaking to any who, like Peter, have denied their Lord? Who perhaps have crucified their Lord afresh in the house of his friends and put him to open shame? Oh, come back to your crucified Lord again! The Father waits to meet and greet you; he waits to put on your cheek the kiss of love and forgiveness.

You see there was an obligation attaching to the fact that Peter had been saved from his wandering, so that he was now to strengthen others. That is God's plan. Whoever receives consolation from God is to comfort others. This duty is not to be done in pride, not in ostentation, but in humility and in simplicity; not to honor yourself, but to glorify God. The bitter experience of wandering gives men power to help others who have wandered. God often overrules our sins that we may help other sinners. If you would know the curse of drunkenness, you cannot learn it fully from me, because I have never known its power; but if I could put into this pulpit a man who has been its victim, his words would have a mighty power. I cannot tell you the awfulness of fire, because I have never been burned; but if I should come to you out of the fire, singed and blackened, I could then tell you of its terrible pain and power. I should know by a personal experience whereof I spoke.

Peter had been grieved at Christ's implied doubt of his fidelity and had protested his own constancy even unto death. But, although he continued for a while with Christ, when the first shade of personal danger fell upon him, he denied him with oaths three times repeated. But a little while after he went out into the gray dawn of the morning, weeping bitterly, and Christ did not see him any more until after the crucifixion and resurrection. If there was a broken-hearted man in Jerusalem during the awful period which followed the denial that man was Peter; and now the resurrection day comes and Christ appears, first to Mary Magdalene and then to the other women, and some time about noon or early afternoon, somewhere, somehow, he appears to Peter. Doubtless Peter was on his mind and in his heart all the morning, for the angel told the women to go and tell the disciples, "and Peter." Who gave the angel this message? Christ out of his loving heart. The Holy Spirit has drawn a veil over Christ's meeting with Peter. Perhaps the meeting was too tender, too sacred for the particulars to be given to the world. Oh, how Peter would fall, weeping penitential tears, at Christ's feet, and how

Christ would forgive, cleanse, and strengthen him. Wonderful moment! Blessed penitence and divine forgiveness! O wanderers, will you go back to Christ this morning? Will you now fall in deep humility at his pierced feet, telling out your penitence and receiving his full and free pardon? Then come back to the church, resume your neglected vows, and take your place at the table of the Lord; begin at once to work for others and thus strengthen the brethren. If some of you have never come to Christ before, come now. He will be your Saviour to-day, your Advocate with the Father, and your Prophet, Priest, and King.

XV

THE PHILIPPIAN PRAYER

"And this I pray, that your love may abound yet more and more in knowledge and in all judgment; that ye may approve things that are excellent; that ye may be sincere and without offence till the day of Christ; being filled with the fruits of righteousness, which are by Christ Jesus, unto the glory and praise of God." Phil. 1: 9–11.

XV

A CAREFUL study of the prayers of the Apostle Paul would certainly be one of the most interesting and instructive lines of Bible study. Whatever doubt there may be as to the use of prayers written by uninspired men, there can be no doubt as to the propriety of frequently using and earnestly studying the prayers of inspired apostles. The simple fact that the text is such a prayer gives us an inspired model of church life. What Paul in his prayer to God desired the Philippian church to be, that we ought to desire the Calvary Church to be. The Apostle Paul was a powerful intercessor at the throne of God. It would much encourage the Philippian church simply to know that he prayed for their spiritual welfare; and the members of that church in reading this prayer would know better how to pray for themselves.

Philippi was famous as the chief city of Macedonia, as taking its name from Philip, the king of Macedon and the father of Alexander the Great, who repaired and beautified it, and as the place of the great battles between Cæsar and Pompey, and also between Augustus and Antony on the one side, and Brutus and Cassius on the other; but to Christians it must ever be most famous for its church and Epistle—a church so beloved by Paul, and an Epistle written when he was a prisoner in Rome, probably about the end of A. D. 62. He cherished a tender regard for that church, both as the earliest fruits of his ministry in Europe, and because of the character and devotion of its members. When the apostle wrote this Epistle he was looking death in the face; he could not hope for much from such a man as Nero. This letter may be his last message to this beloved people. His prayer for them in such circumstances cannot fail to impress itself upon our minds, alike for its practical and spiritual instruction.

1. *He prays that this church may be characterized by an abounding and an intelligent love.* He desired the Philippians to be moral giants. No man has a right to be a moral dwarf. Every man is bound to make the most of himself for God and man, for time and eternity. Every man might live a nobler, a manlier, and a diviner life than most men live. No child of God ought to be satisfied with living in the porter's lodge as a servant, when he might enter the king's palace as a son. This apostolic prayer lifts before us an exalted standard of duty and of possible attainment. The apostle calls God to witness that he entertained for this church the tenderest affection, and that he gave himself

for it with some such love as that which led Christ to give his life for the salvation of the lost. This prayer is probably the substance of many prayers which the apostle offered for this church. In the fourth verse he refers to the fact that in every prayer he made requests with gratitude and joy on their behalf.

He prays now that they should manifest love to God, and that this love should include the entire "fellowship in the gospel," to which fellowship he alludes in the fifth verse. If we do not love our brother whom we have seen, how can we prove that we love God, whom we have not seen? If church-members have all besides, and have not this love, they are poor; if they have it, whatever else they lack, they are rich. In the epistle of the ascended Lord to the Ephesian church the charge is made that they had left their first love. They had much in their life and faith which was commendable. That church had striven against the influence of false teachings; but the spirit of controversy had tended to cool the ardor of their first love toward God and toward one another. The apostle did well, therefore, to pray that the Philippian church should be a loving church. He has elsewhere taught us that love is the fulfilling of the law and also of the gospel; and another apostle has taught us that love covers a multitude of sins. Love is really the new law of the gospel and the epitome of the older law. Luther calls it "the shortest and the longest divinity—short, for the form of words ; long, yea, everlasting, for the use and purpose ; for love shall never cease." And Mr. Beecher, quoting the Apostle Paul's words, "Now, abideth faith, hope, love, these three ; but the greatest of these is love," says, "For love is the seraph, and faith and hope are but the wings by which it flies."

The apostle prays for an increasing love, a love which abounds more and more. It was to be a love which, like a river constantly fed by rain and tributary streams, continues to increase its volume till it fills all its channel, and then floods the adjacent plains. Our best attainments are still very imperfect. They who have most of any grace will desire more ; they who have risen highest are best prepared and most anxious for a loftier flight. They who are satisfied with the grace they have, make it doubtful whether they have any true grace. Although many severe things were charged in the ascended Lord's epistle to the Thyatiran church, it was said concerning their good works that the last were more than the first. So to grow is our duty and privilege to-day. Have we thus grown during the past twenty-two years? Some of you have lived and labored with me in church work during all that period. The number is rapidly decreasing. But three of the constituent members of the church remain, and but about thirty of those who joined hands and hearts with me twenty-two years ago to-day. How strong are the ties that bind us to-day! How sweet the fellowship in which we live and labor! But have we grown as we ought in grace and goodness? In your presence, as in the presence of the omniscient God, I rebuke myself that my growth has not been greater; and yet, with equal honesty, I can thank God that there has been even on my part some growth, as there has been on the part of some of you great growth during that period.

We observe, also, that the apostle prays not only for an increasing, but for an intelligent love on the part of the Philippian church. He prayed that their love might abound more and more "in knowledge and in all judgment" or perception. A blind, impulsive, and unintelligent love is always a doubtful blessing, and is often a positive damage to a church. Love, to be a blessing, must be of the right kind. It must not be separated from knowledge and perception. The emphasis, therefore, is laid on the increase of love in the two particulars named. The apostle desired the people to have clear conceptions of all things related to their duty. They were to understand God's character and perfections and their own relations to him and to their fellow-men. God is to be loved because of the infinite excellence and loveliness of his character; our fellow-men are to be loved because of what we see of the image of God in them even in a state of nature, and much more when they are under the influence of divine grace. There may be a zeal which is not according to knowledge, and such zeal may be a curse rather than a blessing. Love must be associated with a discriminating judgment—such love as might be called moral tact. We ought to pray earnestly for sanctified common sense. God give us grace and love sweetly united to wise knowledge and sound judgment!

2. *The apostle prays that the Philippian church should consist of a discriminating people*—" that ye may approve things that are excellent." This thought follows naturally from that which immediately precedes; it is simply the application of the knowledge and judgment already mentioned. The discriminating faculty in all God's people ought to be in vigorous exercise. They are to learn how to distinguish between things that differ; and, so distinguishing, they are to reject the wrong and choose the right. This thought is implied in the marginal note, and the original word admits that meaning. The word translated approve means "try," and it suggests the kind of trial to which metals are subjected to discover their true nature. The apostle prayed that this church might so test all things

as to discover their real value and to distinguish between the true and the false. They were not to love all things alike; they were not to give their approval indiscriminately. The apostle earnestly desired that they should be intelligent Christians, understanding the real value of all the things upon which they were to pass judgment. Choices determine the man. The man who prefers the daub of the tyro in art to the masterpiece of the experienced artist, writes himself down as inartistic and ignorant. The man who chooses pebbles and rejects diamonds, advertises his folly. What a man habitually chooses, that the man really is. The apostle would have them know Christ, in order that they might be prepared to choose what is Christlike. Indiscriminate approbation is not true charity. The endorsements of men and things which some give are absolutely worthless; to oblige a friend they would endorse anybody or anything. To please one they may thus injure many. While love suffereth long, beareth all things, believeth all things, hopeth all things, endureth all things, it is still true that it "rejoiceth not in iniquity, but rejoiceth in the truth." The man who endorses everything practically endorses nothing. True love is manly, discriminating, and fearless. It will denounce wrong as earnestly as it will declare and approve right. Principles and persons are to be esteemed according to their real worth. Christians need intelligence to guide their convictions and their conduct as truly as they need love to constrain their lives. Such a church as the apostle would have the Philippian church in this respect to be, I to-day would have the Calvary Church to be now and always.

3. *The apostle prayed that they might be a sincere people.* The word translated "sincere" in this connection is very instructive. We shall be repaid for dwelling upon it for a little time. Two derivations of the word have been given, but the one which is the more authoritative makes it "that which is judged of in sunshine," and so that which is clear, pure, and transparent. The word used here in the Greek is used nowhere else in the New Testament except in 2 Peter 3 : 1, and there it is translated pure. There is a noun derived from this word which occurs in several places and which is translated sincerity. The English word sincere is itself worthy of our consideration, although it is not an exact translation of the original Greek word. Every one at all familiar with Latin can readily see that the word sincere is compounded of *sine*, without, and *cera*, wax. When, therefore, you sign a letter, "your sincere friend," you really say, "your friend without wax." That is, without doubt, the meaning of our word sincere. Two explanations of it have been given, one refers it to clarified honey, honey in which no

part of the comb is left; the other refers it to wooden vessels and pieces of furniture in which there were no cracks or knot holes, which have been filled by wax and covered with shellac. It is a solemn thing to sign a letter "your sincere friend." That is truly a noble friendship from which all the wax of pretension has been taken, a friendship in which there are no cracks filled by soft words and smooth speeches. But the original word here means more than our word sincere. The metaphor is taken from the practice of purchasers who carry cloth and other kinds of goods from the darkness of the salesroom into the light of the bright sun that they may the more readily discover any defect which the darkness might conceal. The apostle, therefore, prays that the Philippian church may be so refined and purified, so free from spot or flaw, that even the bright light of God's sunshine falling on their hearts should not reveal any defect. This thought teaches that there ought to be in a Christian nothing deceitful or hypocritical; that he is to be all that he professes, that his life is to be free from trick and cunning, that his motives are to be disinterested and pure, and that he is to be, in a word, like his Lord and Master. Such a character may always be examined in the brightest sunshine of publicity. It is willing to be scanned by men, by angels, and even by God himself. This is a wonderful thought. Who may endure the testing? God help us to possess characters which may be judged in the sunshine here as they shall be judged at the last in the dazzling light of the eternal throne!

4. *The apostle prayed that they might be an inoffensive people.* He would have them without offense until the day of Christ. Perhaps the primary thought here is that they were to be void of offense in the sense that they were not to stumble in their own lives; but the blessing for which the apostle here prayed is two-sided. They were not to be apt to take offense; and they were to be careful not to give offense either to God or to their brethren. They were to live, as the apostle himself had lived, in all good conscience toward God; they were to have a conscience void of offense toward God and toward men. Church-members who are evermore taking offense are a great trial to themselves and to their brethren. Their readiness to notice supposed slights is a confession of conscious weakness. The man whose reputation and character are assured does not stop in his work to imagine that he is slighted. Such a thing does not occur to him. The man who is always so anxious about his social position shows that his social position needs his anxiety. The man who must be careful about his dignity shows that he really has no dignity about which either he or others

should be careful; a dignity which will not take care of itself is not worthy of any man's care. Those who are always looking for slights will be sure to find that for which they look. The man who moves on in the performance of his duty with high aims and holy motives is not likely either to give or to take offense. It is a blessed thing to be able to do one's whole duty without fear or favor and yet to lead a blameless life. Some may depreciate this attainment as being only a negative virtue; but we really pay a man a very high compliment when we say that he is without offense toward all men, both in his conversation and in his example. This so-called negative virtue thus becomes a positive power for good. Men of great talent are often shorn of power for good because of their offensiveness in word and in deed. There are men who make long strides to-day in the right direction, and to-morrow, by unfortunate words or acts, take it all back and are no farther on in the Christian race than they were before the long strides were taken. The man who strikes ten to-day for Christ and who will strike ten to-morrow against him, cannot, of course, make progress in divine things. The man who never strikes more than five, but always strikes five for Christ, will be an honor to the Master and an unspeakable blessing to the world. This inoffensive life must be continued until the day of Christ; and then he will present his church without spot or wrinkle faultless before the presence of his glory with exceeding joy.

5. *The apostle further prays that this might be a fruitful church*—" being filled with the fruits of righteousness, which are by Jesus Christ, unto the glory and praise of God." The thought of this part of the prayer is that these Philippians should manifest in daily life those fruits which righteousness in the heart produces. True religion is evermore progressive; the whole man, body, soul, and spirit, is to come under its power and to be filled with its influence. True faith in the heart evermore works outward in fruits of honesty, charity, and practical godliness. If the root of the matter is in us the fruit of holiness will be borne by us. Righteousness in the heart must manifest itself by rightness in the life. True religion cannot be concealed. A religion which a man can hide is a religion not worth having or hiding. If the "Rose of Sharon" is in your bosom, its fragrance will fill the whole circle in which you move. We are to be filled, rounded out, completed, perfected with the fruits of righteousness. The more religion you give out the more you have; the more you keep the less you have. These fruits of righteousness result from Christ's indwelling in the heart and from his power over the life. He is the root of the divine olive from which the fatness and

strength of our love come. If there is no fruit in the life we may rest assured that Christ is not really in the heart; for it is his will that we bear much fruit. He is most honored when his people most abound in good works.

Dear to the heart of the apostle was this Philippian church. For its growth in grace he poured out his heart in this tender and fervent prayer. Dear to your pastor's heart is this Calvary Church. With all the faults and failings on his part which have marked these twenty-two years, he can honestly say in the presence of God and his people that he loves this church, and that its prosperity and the honor of our common Master are the strongest desire of his heart. The pastor cannot but think to-day of the noble men and saintly women with whom twenty-two years ago he joined in the work and worship of this church, and who to-day are in the immediate presence of Christ, rejoicing in the beatific vision for which often on earth their souls longed. They to-day have attained a more perfect character than that for which the apostle prayed for the Philippian church. We still remain. Our hearts are bound in sweetest fellowship and in truest loyalty to one another and to Christ. Let this love be without dissimulation; let this love abide; let this love have even here a foretaste of that blessedness which will be its full fruition in heaven. With gratitude we glance over the past; with consecration we look at the present; with hope we turn to the future. With a consuming love to Jesus Christ as the constraining motive we lay hold of new duties and press forward to win new triumphs.

I stand here to-day at the close of twenty-two years to reaffirm with increasing emphasis my faith in the distinctive principles of our beloved denomination. With advancing years, with wider experience, and with greater opportunities for historic and linguistic examination, I declare my earlier faith without a qualification, and with growing certainty. During these years we have seen the Episcopal Church greatly disturbed over its internal management, over its opposing wings, and over the revision of its prayer book. We to-day see the Presbyterian Church shaken to its center over discussions regarding the orthodoxy of some of its theological professors, over the relation of some of its theological seminaries to the church, and over its Confession of Faith. But we stand to-day practically a unit, notwithstanding our great numbers, in our loyalty to the word of God, as the only rule of faith and practice. All the great movements alike in the political and religious world are endorsing our views regarding the separation of Church and State, regarding the importance of individuality in the Christian profession, and regarding the supremacy of the word of God in the case of all who are consistent Protestants. During these years I have seen great movements in the direction of municipal reform. We have had ever and anon spurts of heroism and spasms of virtue, and after a little time we have seen the evil rampant as before. I do not antagonize any of these movements. I believe with Mr. Gladstone, that we ought to make vice as difficult and virtue as easy as possible. I believe that we ought to employ every instrumentality, legal as well as moral, for the overthrow of evil and for the triumph of good. But I am more than ever convinced that the one hope of this lost world is in the gospel of Christ as seen in the regeneration of individual souls. This seems to many a hopelessly slow method of reform. Many wish to introduce great moral mowing machines, and they are impatient with the gospel sickle; but Christ's method is still the true method. In proportion to the population, there was as much evil in the world in his day as there is in our day. His one great method of reform he announced when he said, "Preach the gospel to every creature." When lost men and women are regenerated by the grace of God through the gospel of Christ we close the fountain whence streams of evil flow. We shall then close all evil resorts, because we shall have robbed them of their patronage and support.

On the twenty-fifth anniversary of his pastorate in London, the great modern Babylon, Mr. Spurgeon spoke brave and loving words of his faith in the old gospel of the Son of God. In my greatly humbler measure and position I would adopt his thought and adapt his words to the circumstances of this hour. For two and twenty years I have stood in this city beside the cross of Jesus Christ, believing that his gospel is still the power of God unto salvation to every one that believeth, and should God spare my life for two and twenty years more I shall have no other place in which to stand, and no other truth to preach.

XVI

THE TRIUMPHANT WORSHIPERS

S

"And round about the throne were four and twenty thrones; and upon the thrones I saw four and twenty elders sitting, arrayed in white garments; and on their heads crowns of gold." Rev. 4 : 4.

XVI

THIS text forms a part of the chapter which begins the series of remarkable symbolic visions which are characteristic of the book of Revelation. Glorious is the vision with which this chapter opens; it is a sublime theophany, or manifestation of the great God. The Apostle John is permitted to look into heaven, and upon the throne he sees God, and about him devout worshipers. In the twenty-four enthroned elders we are to see representatives of the church militant and triumphant. The number twenty-four is perhaps an allusion to the twenty-four courses of Jewish priests; their white raiment is emblematic of purity, and their crowns of gold represent the kingly office which they sustain, and also suggest that they had been faithful unto death, and so were rewarded with crowns of life. It is perhaps not too violent an accommodation for us to-day to see in these twenty-four kingly priests and priestly kings, who have triumphed over earthly foes and who are now participants of heavenly glory, a suggestion of the twenty-four years of church work through which as pastor and people we have been permitted to pass.

Certain features of the work during these twenty-four years are worthy of mention on this occasion. The remarks already made suggest one characteristic of the work of this church during this period; that feature is set forth in one word—"*Christism.*" This word is not found in dictionaries, but it is correctly formed, and its meaning has been emphasized during the ministry which to-day closes its twenty-fourth and begins its twenty-fifth year. Christ has been enthroned in our prayers, purposes, and precepts. The aim has been to make his will the law of our lives. This ministry was begun with the distinct determination to continue and to end it in harmony with the universal and eternal law formulated by our Lord when he said, " He that findeth his life shall lose it ; and he that loseth his life for my sake shall find it." All life worthy of the name finds its highest inspiration and noblest endeavors in self-sacrifice. Living for ourselves, we die ; but living for Christ, we live rightly here and shall live joyously forever hereafter. Not self, but Christ, must be enthroned in heart and home and church, if our lives are to be nobly spent. Christ is enthroned everywhere in the word of God. It is the fullest revelation of God's will ever made to man ; it is the sublimest declaration of the eternal law of God revealed for the government of human conduct. The ancient shield whose maker's name was so inwrought in its parts that to remove the name was to destroy the shield, sets forth the revelation of Jesus Christ in the Bible. He is the glory of creation's song, the theme of prophetic ecstasy, the object of the believer's faith, and the foundation of his hope, and he will be the inspiration of our song forever in heaven. No one can share the throne of revelation, the throne of experience, the throne of redemption, and the throne of a true churchism with Jesus Christ. This pulpit cannot sympathize with the remark recently made, according to newspaper report, by a Roman priest at a public meeting in this city, that "the Roman Church had put the Virgin Mary on an equality with her redeeming Son, Jesus Christ." Christ alone is king; in his pierced hand he holds the helm of the universe, and his will alone is law in Zion. The true apostolic church is that church whose ordinances and practices are most in harmony with the will of Jesus Christ as laid down in the New Testament. He never can accept our divided allegiance; he can never share with a creature, a creed, a theology, his glorious throne. All these twenty-four years fall down to-day before Jesus Christ, casting their crowns at his feet, and saying: "Thou art worthy, O Lord, to receive glory, and honor, and power; for thou hast created all things, and for thy pleasure they are and were created." May the love of Christ constrain us joyously, heroically, triumphantly, to run after him in the path of obedience on earth, and finally to serve him day and night in his heavenly temple!

Another characteristic of the aim of this ministry is *Humanism*. This word is designedly chosen; humanism may be defined as a system of thought or effort in which human interests are prominent, if not predominant. There is no contradiction between a controlling Christism and a predominant humanism. Jesus Christ was divine, and yet Jesus Christ was also human. In the incarnation of Christ the divine was humanized that the human might be divinized. Humanization on his part, so far as we can see, was necessary to divinization on our part. Christ inserted himself into our race at its lowest and weakest point; the church in like manner must insert herself, with all her heavenly ministries, all her beneficent devotions, and all her divine inspirations, into the race to-day where it is weakest, saddest, and sinfulest. If Christ was to lift the race it was necessary that he should place himself beneath it; if the church to-day is to lift men she must place herself beneath them. We never can do effective work for Christ at long ranges. We need to-day what has been finely called, "an enthusiasm for humanity." The world and the church, in a divinely beautiful sense, must come closer together.

If the sacred salt is to save the secular meat they must not be put into separate barrels. When Jesus helped men who were blind, he touched their eyes; men who were deaf, he put his finger in their ears; men who had fallen low, he lifted them up with his own hand. So the church now must have a great heart of love, and a warm, strong hand of help for those who are down in sorrow and sin. It will not do for the church simply to send her check or her missionaries into the abodes of wretchedness and sinfulness; she must go herself in the person of her manly sons and her consecrated daughters.

A Roman theater, we are told, burst forth with sincere and enthusiastic applause at the pronouncement of the words of Terence, "I am a man, and I deem nothing common to man foreign to me." The church of Jesus Christ must say to-day, "I am redeemed, that I may redeem; I am won by grace divine, that I, with divine help, may win many trophies to Jesus Christ." The church needs a broader, deeper, truer, and so holier conception of her mission. She must be like her Lord, always about her Father's business; she must strive so to think and act that eating and drinking, buying and selling, working and worshiping, shall be all done to the glory of God. There is no interest of the human race to which she can afford to be indifferent; she must gird herself for the lowliest services inspired by the loftiest motives. It is possible for the church thus to consecrate herself to all human interests without losing the purity of her purpose, the sweetness of her spirit, or the Christliness of her motive. Indeed, she can retain these divine characteristics only by consecrating herself, as did her Lord, to holy service for sinners who most need her angelic ministry. Great sociological, political, and religious problems are pressing upon the attention of the church for her consideration; and more and more must she learn that her noblest liturgy is in following her Lord, "who went about doing good."

Another desired characteristic in this ministry can be expressed by the word *Patriotism*. It is true of all Christians that they are citizens of another country, even an heavenly; but they are none the less citizens of the country that now is, and which at times is painfully earthly. The nobler their devotion religiously, the more loyal should their aim be patriotically. There is really no contradiction between sincere patriotism to the American Republic, and profound devotion to the heavenly kingdom. Perhaps we ought not to take politics, in the technical sense, into our religion; but it is very certain that we ought to take religion, in the practical sense, into our politics. The man who cannot take his religion into his politics must have very bad politics or very poor religion, or both. I have great sympathy with Samuel Johnson when he said: "That man is little to be envied whose patriotism would not gain force upon the plain of Marathon, or whose piety would not grow warmer among the ruins of Iona." So every true American in reviewing the history of his country, will find cause for an increase of patriotism and of piety, as he traces the dealings of God with the land of his birth or of his adoption. The pulpit has too much neglected its duty in relation to the advocacy of pure politics and of nobler statesmanship. We should oftener, in our sermons, illustrate the spirit of President Lincoln's last inaugural, in which he recognizes, as did Washington in his first inaugural, the hand of God in the history of the nation. Both of these great presidents emphasized the duty of honoring God as the preserver of all the sacred interests of the American people. Though often misquoted as an unbeliever, Thomas Jefferson, at the close of his inaugural, also expresses his need of "the favor of that Being in whose hands we all are; and who led our fathers as Israel of old"; in additional words, equally expressive of faith in God, he asked the people to join with him in supplication for God's continued favor.

We are glad that not for nearly a generation have the citizens of this great metropolis been so alive as to-day to their humiliation before the civilized world because of the political degradation of the city of New York.

This pulpit has uttered earnest warnings against the dangers of Romanism considered as an ecclesiastico-political machine. Of individual Romanists no unkind words are spoken; the Roman Church, as a religious teacher, it is not the purpose, in this connection, to criticise. Criticism of that character is appropriate in its place; but this pulpit has spoken only of that system in its relations to the degradation of politics and the subversion of a true American patriotism. Romanism is largely responsible for all the perils to which this republic is exposed. It would be easy for me to quote some of its own priests, giving their exact words, who admit that an enormously large proportion of drunkards and drunkard-makers belong to that church. When has the Roman Church ever uttered words against the saloon half as bitter as it has pronounced against our public schools? Does that church hate the saloons as much as it hates the schools? We are not troubled with the immigrants who come from England, from Scotland, from the north of Ireland, and from Scandinavia; but our chief difficulty arises in connection with those who come from papal Ireland, from Italy, Poland, Hungary, Austria, and other countries under the rule of the papacy.

Is not that church also largely responsible for our municipal misgovernment? Look at our own city and receive an affirmative answer to my question. Its officers, from the acting and the real mayor down to its charwomen are, for the most part, members of that church. I am glad to say that not all Romanists are the enemies of true patriotism; some are large-hearted, patriotic, and genuinely American. But, it will scarcely be denied that their American patriotism is often at the expense of their Roman consistency. But there are Jesuits who are the enemies of any country; driven from several European countries by rulers who are themselves Roman in faith, they have come stealthily to this land to subvert our American institutions. They are men who know no country but their church, no flag but that of the papacy, no law but their own order and their ecclesiastical superiors; they are men who have no recognized families but their sodalities and other fraternities. They are ever grasping after political power in order to secure ecclesiastical dominance. In this connection it is to be said that every patriot must to-day heartily oppose the giving of public moneys for sectarian institutions. During the year 1893, from the general and the excise funds, the Roman Church in the city of New York has received $1,213,000; and all the Protestant bodies have received but $75,000.

Appropriations from the national treasury for sectarian instruction among the Indians violate both the spirit and letter of the Constitution of the United States. The Roman and the Mormon Churches are united in attempting to destroy the time-honored American principle of separation between Church and State. Romanism has gone too far; the American people are aroused, and have declared that Rome shall no farther go. Already the eastern sky is colored with the crimson and gold of a brighter day.

Another characteristic of our work is what may be called *Churchism*. Churchism is earnest adherence to the principles or practices of some church. The word church is employed with much latitude of meaning. We know that in the New Testament it was applied to spiritual bodies called out and separated from the multitude, and who were united together for Christian work and worship; but the word has come to be applied also to a building used for Christian worship, and to Christians in given communities or countries. There is a churchism which is dangerous to all true spiritual life and power. There is a churchianity which is often opposed to a true Christianity; but there is a golden mean between a secular religious organization and an undue exaltation of the church.

We attach no undue importance to the mere building consecrated to the service of God; but there is a sense in which such a building stands apart from all other structures. It is frankly admitted that in the early history of Christianity churches flourished when the people had no houses consecrated to the worship of God; nevertheless we ought to give due honor to the house and worship of God. One aim of this ministry has been to exalt the services of public worship by making them scriptural, churchly, and, in a right sense, æsthetic; all the people have had the opportunity to join audibly in parts of the worship. The word of God has been honored in the public worship by responsive readings, and by having the Bible in the hands of every worshiper. Churches whose ritual is prescribed by external ecclesiastical authority have no liberty of choice, and no opportunity for the exercise of taste, or for adaptation to local necessities. Fortunately we are not under such restraint; all that is best in every church and in every century is ours, so far as our necessity requires and our taste suggests. All that is noblest in song and ritual, in litany and liturgy, is ours. We deny that any church has a monopoly of ecclesiastical symbolism and sacred liturgy. We have made our selection from the best which the history of Christianity has produced. Our polity admits of the exercise of this Christian liberty, under the direction of cultivated taste and sanctified endeavor. There may be a dangerous ritualism in the use of the baldest forms of service; ritualism really consists in excessive devotion to forms, however plain, bald, and barren. Its essence is not in the nature of the ritual itself, but rather in the unwise exaltation of that ritual, as if it were given by inspiration of God, and so authoritatively binding on the churches of Christ. We have also honored loyal devotion to the principles and practices of our Baptist faith, which we believe to be truly catholic and genuinely apostolic. Granting the largest liberty for others, we have claimed for ourselves the duty and privilege of loyalty to Jesus Christ as his will is made known in the New Testament. This is a true churchism; whatever is more, whatever is less, is a perverted churchism. We desire ever to affirm that Jesus Christ is king in Zion, and that his word is the authoritative manual for his true disciples.

A last characteristic of which mention will be made is *Unionism*. No undivided vote has ever been taken in this church; no root of bitterness has ever sprung up in our church life; but peace and prosperity, harmony and unity, enthusiasm and devotion, have marked all our private deliberations and all our public endeavors. We have realized that we are to fight against the world, the flesh, and the devil, and not against one another. The unity of the Spirit in the bonds of peace has ever characterized our relations; and for this blessing we to-day devoutly thank Almighty God, and for its continuance we earnestly labor and pray. All the members of this church are brothers; the interests of each are the interests of all. When one brother suffers, all suffer with him. Our beautiful church covenant teaches us that we are to pray one for another, that we are to seek one another's welfare, and that we are to comfort one another in sickness and in distress. This Calvary Church is not the church of the rich; it is not the church of the poor. But it is the church of both rich and poor. At God's altar none are rich, none are poor; there all are brethren. The church of Christ, properly understood, gives us the noblest illustration of a true liberty, equality, and fraternity. This church has a warm hand and a loving heart for all young men and women, and older men and women, coming as strangers to our great city. It desires to generate and to diffuse the spirit of welcome in all its services.

Twenty-four years ago this morning, when the first sermon of this pastorate was preached, the text was, "Bear ye one another's burdens, and so fulfill the law of Christ." It was designed that this text should strike the keynote of the present pastorate; to some degree that design has been realized and that purpose accomplished. Here, literally, thousands of young men and young women have found a church home; and from this home many have gone out to fill honored places in the varied walks of life, and to be beloved and consecrated members of other churches. The design is that all our services should be restful, uplifting, inspiring, and Christly; we labor and pray that here thousands may cast their burdens on the Lord, and may learn that he sustains, inspires, and forgives. We desire to have Christ in the midst of every worshiping assembly, and ever to hear his gracious benediction, " Peace be with you." We have striven to justify the sweet promise carved before your eyes, " In this place will I give peace." The pastor and all the other officers of this church joyfully and gladly proclaim themselves to be your friends, brethren, and servants " In His Name."

We have nothing whereof to boast, but we have much, very much, for which to be deeply and tenderly thankful. No words can express the thankful thoughts that are in my heart to-day. Never shall I cease to be grateful for those who began with me, and who are now in heaven, and also that God has spared other noble men and women to work with me all through these years, and to be by my side to-day as my beloved friends and efficient helpers. Our fellowship has been sweetened by sorrow, softened by tears, and cemented by prayers. Grateful to God am I for the new friends who have come among us during these years, and for some of my truest helpers who have come quite recently. What has the future in store for us? God alone knows, and we ask not to know; enough for us that to-day we lay ourselves joyously at the pierced feet of the Lord Jesus, with a fuller consecration, a tenderer devotion, and a more Christly love than we have ever known.

The day is coming when we ourselves shall be enthroned, robed in white, and with crowns of gold upon our heads, looking upon him who sits upon the throne, and at whose feet we shall cast our crowns, saying: "Blessing and honor, and glory and power, be unto him that sitteth upon the throne and unto the Lamb for ever and ever."

XVII

THE JUBILEE YEAR
(1847–1897)

"And ye shall hallow the fiftieth year . . . It shall be a jubilee unto you." . . . *Lev. 25 : 10.*

XVII

THE Jubilee Festival was one of the most interesting of Hebrew institutions. Its celebration occurred on every fiftieth year. Its occurrence was, as many authorities agree, the year after seven weeks of years, or seven times seven years. Its name refers to the flowing, sounding, joyous peals of the trumpets which announced its return. During the jubilee year there was neither sowing nor reaping; by permitting the land to lie fallow for a year the fertility of the soil was greatly increased, the people living meanwhile on the provision which remained from the abundance of preceding years. All of the possessions that had been sold, mortgaged, or otherwise alienated, were restored to their original owners; and all Hebrew servants were set free, with their wives and children. Various festivities prevailed during the first nine days of the jubilee and no one worked during that time, and many of the people wore crowns, indicative of the regal joy which they experienced. The tenth day was the day of solemn expiation. On that day the Sanhedrin ordered the trumpets to sound, and with the sound of the trumpets slaves were declared free, and the land was returned to its hereditary owners. The year of cessation of work gave parents the opportunity for instructing their children in the history and religion of their fathers. The great lesson of the jubilee was that God was really the owner and dispenser of all things, and that the people were his tenants and stewards, under bonds to render an accounting to him. Isaiah refers to this jubilee as illustrating the benefits of the gospel dispensation during the period of the Messiah. It finds, therefore, its fullest spiritual significance even in our own time.

To-day, in the providence of God, the Calvary Church celebrates its jubilee. We meet on a higher tableland of fraternal equality with one another and of filial relationship with God than did the ancient Hebrews. The jubilee has its glorious realization under Jesus Christ, who came to give liberty to the captive, to preach the gospel to the poor, to heal the broken-hearted, to give sight to the blind, and to preach the acceptable year of the Lord. Life is measured by deeds not by years. We live longer now in fifty years than did Methusaleh in his nine hundred and sixty-nine years. Well has Bailey, in his "Festus," said :

> We live in deeds, not years ; in thoughts, not breaths ;
> In feelings, not in figures on a dial.
> We should count time by heart throbs ; he most lives
> Who thinks most, feels the noblest, acts the best."

The most important period of its length in the whole history of the human race is the last half-century. One may read the history of all Oriental countries, the history of Greece and Rome, of Italy and Spain, of France and Germany, of Great Britain and her colonies, and the preceding history of the United States, without finding any other half-century in which so many great political, social, moral, and religious questions were earnestly asked and rightly answered, as during the last fifty years. During this period we have seen Italy united into one kingdom with Victor Emmanuel II., first king of United Italy, riding in triumph through the streets of the Eternal City; we have seen the temporal power of the pope destroyed and never to be restored; we have seen all Germany consolidated into a compact empire; we have seen France humiliated and Germany triumphant on French soil; we have seen France recuperate with a rapidity as gratifying as it is surprising; we have seen over forty millions of serfs liberated in Russia, and four millions of slaves translated from bondage into freedom in America, as one of the results of the greatest civil war in the history of the world; and we have heard the song of liberty rolling across the continent from the mighty Atlantic to the mightier Pacific, girdling the world and ascending to heaven with the music of many oceans as its sublime accompaniment. We have seen such progress in art, science, and literature, and in the application of religious principles to human necessities, as the world never before saw, and such as the world scarcely ever dared expect. Since this church was founded virtually a new world has been created.

1. This ought to be a day of jubilee for us because of God's mercies to this our beloved Calvary Church. It is most interesting that the church was organized on this very date, February 28, 1847. As early as November, 1846, Rev. David Bellamy resigned the office of pastor of the Stanton Street Church, and action was immediately taken by some of his friends to organize another church. A meeting for that purpose was called at 219 Wooster Street, New York, November 25, 1847. The night was dark and stormy, and only ten persons were present; a few evenings later another meeting was held and, although there were only fourteen persons present, an organization was effected under the name of the Hope Chapel Congregation. The Coliseum, a public hall at 450 Broadway, was secured as the place of public worship, and David Bellamy was invited to preach on the following Sunday. On Sunday, January 3, 1847, a meeting was held and resolutions were passed looking to the organization of an independent Baptist church.

We now come to Sunday, February 28, fifty years ago to-day. The people on that day were invited to remain at the close of the evening service. Rev. Elisha Tucker, pastor of the Oliver Street Baptist Church, who was present by invitation, was elected chairman of the meeting. Rev. David Bellamy presented the preamble and resolution which, when adopted, constituted those present into a Baptist church under the title of "The Hope Chapel Baptist Church in the city of New York." The adoption of this resolution was followed by the adoption of the Articles of Faith common in Baptist churches. Then one hundred and seven former members of the Stanton Street Church, or of other Baptist churches, subscribed their names, and an official call was extended to Rev. David Bellamy to become the pastor of the church thus organized. The Hope Chapel Church was recognized on April 22, 1847, by a council called for that purpose, composed of delegates from neighboring Baptist churches, and which met at the First Baptist Church, on Broome Street. The motion to receive it was made by the distinguished Spencer H. Cone, D. D., at that time pastor of the First Baptist Church. On the evening of the First Sunday in May following, the public services of recognition were held in the Coliseum, James L. Hodge, D. D., then pastor of the First Baptist Church, Brooklyn, preaching the sermon, Rev. Elisha Tucker giving the hand of fellowship, and Rev. C. G. Somers delivering the address to the church.

The first pastor, as we have seen, was Rev. David Bellamy. He was born at Kingsbury, Washington County, N. Y., and was descended from New England stock, the first American Bellamy being one of the original settlers of New Haven. Rev. Dr. Joseph Bellamy, whose writings with those of Jonathan Edwards, did so much to give shape to New England theology, was his great-grandfather. In 1849 he resigned the pastorate of the Calvary Church, and finally accepted a call to the First Baptist Church of Rome, N. Y., where he spent the last years of his life. On the first of October, 1864, while returning from a funeral, he was stricken with apoplexy and died in a few hours. He did not have all the advantages of a collegiate course of training, but he was a careful student, an able preacher, and a consecrated workman in the Lord's vineyard.

The second pastor was John Dowling, D. D., who assumed the charge of the church January 23, 1850, but resigned April 13, 1852. Doctor Dowling was born at Pavensey, England, May 12, 1807. In 1832 he came to America. He was twice pastor of the Berean Church, in New York City. He was widely known as the author of a "History of Romanism," nearly thirty thousand copies of which have been sold. He was a man of warm impulses; and to a prolific mind and a generous heart he united a character of high rectitude. He died at Middletown, N. Y., July, 1878.

On August 1, 1852, A. D. Gillette, D. D., was called. It seems strange to us to-day that a meeting to call a pastor should have been held on August 1; but the work of the churches was not so largely abandoned then in summer as it is in our day. During Doctor Gillette's pastorate the lots on Twenty-third Street were bought, and the church erected thereon. It was with difficulty that he could induce the brethren of that day to go so far uptown as Twenty-third Street. The lots cost eighteen thousand dollars, and they were sold by us in 1883 for two hundred and twenty-five thousand dollars. The church on Twenty-third Street was opened for worship on the first Sunday in May, 1854, the people having worshiped for some months previous in the basement. The total cost of erecting and furnishing the church was about fifty-five thousand dollars. In September, 1854, the name was changed to the Calvary Baptist Church. It was greatly wise to give the church a name significant and beautiful in itself, and not a name dependent on location; such names are never appropriate, and often they are entirely misleading. The South Church, for example, was for a time one of the most northern, and the North Church one of the most southern of our churches in the city. Great were the struggles of the people in those early days; only by heroic efforts were the current expenses paid and the debt somewhat reduced. On December 22, 1863, Doctor Gillette resigned his pastorate, which thus extended over a period of more than eleven years. Afterward he took up his abode in Washington, D. C. In those terrible days of the Civil War, after the fight with General Early, at Fort Stevens, Doctor Gillette found work in going from hospital to hospital, and from camp to camp, caring for the wounded and dying. He was often employed as chaplain for both Houses of Congress. At the request of President Johnson and Secretary Stanton, he spent much time during the last days of their lives with the conspirators who assassinated President Lincoln. The case of Paine especially interested him, because of his acquaintance with and regard for Paine's father. In December, 1868, he utterly broke down during the Communion service; then came a period of rest and travel abroad. While in London he enjoyed the intimate friendship of Mr. Spurgeon, Hon. and Rev. Baptist Noel, and other distinguished men in different denominations. In May, 1880, while attending the Baptist National Anniversaries at Saratoga, he was stricken with apoplexy. On May 29,

1882, a long-cherished wish was gratified, he being able to be present at the laying of the corner-stone of this edifice. August 24, 1882, he calmly fell asleep at his summer home at Lake George, in his seventy-fifth year. Doctor Gillette was one of the most loving and lovable of men. His memory still lives in the hearts of all whose good fortune it was to know him as friend and pastor. His funeral service was held in the old Calvary Church, on Monday, August 28, 1882. Doctors Samson, Burlingham, Armitage, Everts, Scott, and Deems, together with the pastor of the church, participated in the services.

The next pastor was R. J. W. Buckland, D. D., who was called November 1, 1864. September 24, 1869, he resigned, and accepted the chair of church history in the Rochester Theological Seminary. During the pastorate of Doctor Buckland, through the wise counsels, inspiring leadership, and generous example of Nathan Bishop, LL. D., Mr. Ebenezer Cauldwell, and others, the large balance of the debt was paid. Doctor Buckland died in 1877, in the city of Rochester.

The present pastor entered upon his work May 15, 1870. The events of the twenty-fifth anniversary of his pastorate are fresh in the minds of all. His yoke-fellows have been Rev. J. B. Calvert, Rev. John Love, Rev. Joseph Weston, Rev. E. D. Simons, and Frank Rogers

Morse, D. D., with all of whom he has labored in the most delightful spirit of fraternal fellowship.

The corner-stone of our present church home was laid May 29, 1882. Services were first held in the chapel, July 8, 1883, and in the church proper December 23, 1883. A full description of the church and chapel, with all their significant symbolism, is found in the "History of the Calvary Baptist Church," published a few years ago. The number of members baptized into the fellowship of the church is exactly two thousand. The entire number received by baptism, experience, and restoration, four thousand two hundred and sixteen. The present number is nearly two thousand. The church has given the majority of members to two new churches recently formed and is thus a mother of churches in New York City. Its members have also started new churches in neighboring cities and towns. The church has been active in all forms of mission work at home and abroad during all the years of its history. It has contributed for the carrying on of its own immediate work, including the cost of the present church, and also for home and foreign missions, more than two million dollars. The present church and site cost five hundred and twenty-five thousand dollars; of this sum two hundred and twenty-five thousand dollars was received from the sale of the property on Twenty-third Street, and the balance of three hundred thousand dollars was contributed by the people, there being now no debt on the property. We now need to move forward and secure lots, and as soon as possible erect a suitable house of worship for the Calvary Branch, now meeting in the chapel on Sixty-eighth Street and the Boulevard. The banner over us has been love during all the years of our history.

2. This ought to be a time of jubilee for us because of the growth, during the past half-century, of the great denomination of which we form a part. When this church was organized in 1847, the population of the United States was in round numbers twenty millions. The number of regular Baptists in the United States at that time was a little less than six hundred and sixty thousand. The population of the United States to-day (1897) is, perhaps, sixty-seven millions, and the number of Baptists to-day is nearly four millions; if we include the various bodies which are Baptists, so far as baptism is concerned, the number is considerably over five millions. Half a century ago Baptists were but one in thirty of the population; to-day we are about one in seventeen of the population. Our gain is not due, as is that of the Roman, the Episcopal, the Lutheran, and the Presbyterian churches, to any appreciable degree, to immigration; it is chiefly due to the natural growth of our churches among

the people of American birth. During this period the population of the country has not increased three and one-half times, but the membership of our Baptist churches has increased about six times. This is certainly a remarkable growth, and is cause for great gratitude to God for his wonderful mercies to us as a people. Our growth has not been proportionately great in the City of New York. Here it is extremely difficult to stem the tide of influences adverse to our progress. A very great population in this city is foreign; among that population we cannot expect much growth. There is also constantly a very considerable emigration from the city. Nevertheless we have pushed forward with commendable zeal and with encouraging results.

During the last twenty-five years our growth in educational matters has been remarkable. Twenty-five years ago the amount of property and endowment belonging to our colleges and theological seminaries was not more than three and a half millions; to-day it is not less than thirty-seven millions. The growth of the University of Chicago is one of the great events in our recent history as a people. During the last twenty years we have more than doubled the number of our ministers. For several years there has been a net gain of about one hundred thousand in the membership of our churches; a thousand in the number of our churches; and an increase of over eight hundred ministers each year. These facts are not mentioned in a spirit of boastfulness, but in profound gratitude to God for his wonderful blessings to us as a people.

3. This ought to be a jubilee to us all because of the great progress of missions and of civil and religious liberty throughout the world. The past fifty years have witnessed a growth in missions in all parts of the world such as no prophet in the beginning of the half-century would have dared foretell. Then many great countries were entirely closed to the gospel; now their doors are thrown wide open and missionaries are urgently invited to enter. The gospel is girdling the globe with the blessings of salvation. Some evangelists have recently uttered pessimistic wails over the degenerate condition of the churches and the decadent influence of the pulpit. Never were men more utterly mistaken than are these peripatetic Jeremiahs. It would seem as if they were endeavoring to fit the facts to their theories regarding the speedy coming of Christ, and the waxing worse and worse of the world until the return of the Messiah. There is no department of life into which we can look but that we see signs of wonderful progress at every point. Never were the churches more vigorous in home and foreign mission work than they are to-day. It is true that we do not have

the great spasmodic revivals of half a century ago, but the additions to the churches are now far greater than they were at that time. It is true that church work at home and mission work abroad is suffering now somewhat from the extraordinary financial stringency of the times; but these depressed times are not to continue long, as we rightly believe and as we certainly hope. There is a higher standard of morals today regarding temperance, regarding lotteries, and almost all social questions than a half-century ago. Then many great churches were built from the deep foundation stone to the lofty cross with the proceeds of great lotteries. Then colleges were endowed by the profits of lotteries, and college presidents managed the lotteries for the benefit of their colleges "and the glory of God." It is an interesting fact, which the pessimist ought to bear in mind, that the gifts of the churches during the year 1896 in special contributions were very much greater than in 1895. The recent gift of two hundred and fifty thousand dollars by one of our own denominational brethren to remove the debt from our missionary societies is a wonderful illustration of generosity on behalf of missions.

Men talk about "the good old days." Just what days do they mean? Do they refer to the times when Baptists were whipped in the streets of Boston; the time when students were excluded from Yale College for the sin of attending a Baptist church during their vacation; the time when Baptists were brutally persecuted in Virginia? Do they refer to the time when intemperance was so common in the churches that so distinguished a man as Leonard Woods, D. D., says: "I remember when I could reckon up among my acquaintances forty ministers who were intemperate." Another gentleman, living in those early times, subsequently said in a Boston newspaper: "A great many deacons in New England died drunkards. I have a list of one hundred and twenty-three intemperate deacons in Massachusetts, forty-three of whom became sots." Rev. Joseph Badger, as late as 1803, tells us that Cleveland, O., had no church, and "infidelity and Sabbath profanation were general." A gentleman visiting western New York in 1798 said: "Religion has not got west of the Genesee River. Some towns are hotbeds of infidelity." There were then but few students in our great American colleges who were professing Christians; now there are few who are not. These are wonderful days in which we live. There is far less infidelity in every walk in life than there was fifty, or even twenty-five, years ago, and it is very much less defiant and dominant than it was at that time. Let no one's heart fail him because of present discussions regarding the interpretation and inspiration of the Bible. We can still say, as Browning sings in "Pippa Passes":

> God's in his heaven—
> All's right with the world!

It is not in the interest of Satan that this is an age of railroads, electricity, telegraphs, telephones, and labor-saving machinery of every kind; it is not in the interest of Satan that while in 1810 it cost one hundred and twenty-five dollars to haul a ton of goods from Philadelphia to Pittsburg it now costs but a few cents; it is not in the interest of Satan that whereas, in the early part of the century there were no envelopes, no postage stamps, no letter boxes, no collection nor delivery of mails, we now have all these things in great abundance. About three-quarters of a century ago the postage on a letter from New York to Washington was twenty-five cents. The cities were at that time unpaved, unlighted, unsewered, and their water supply was derived from wells and cisterns, often the breeding-place of disease. A little more than half a century ago smallpox and yellow fever ravaged New York, Philadelphia, and Baltimore year after year. Fifty years ago New York had a population of about four hundred and fifty thousand. Brooklyn, whose population is now nearly one million, was then not one-tenth as large as now—it was then about as large as Albany is to-day. In 1840, Chicago was actually a village, and in 1850 but little larger than one of our minor municipalities. During this half-century, New York has virtually been rebuilt; its streets have been repaved and its sanitary regulations so improved as to drive out epidemic diseases. Now its poorest dwellings are protected by scientific plumbing against dangers to life and health. In spite of the rapid increase in population, and that largely by immigration, there are proportionately fewer breaches of the peace now than half a century ago. Once elections were occasions for violent ebullitions and bloodshed; now they take place as peacefully as if election day were a village Sunday. Gangs of ruffians are far less numerous than they were fifty years ago. The city is physically and morally far more wholesome than it was half a century ago. With all New York's faults, we love this city with true loyalty as she sits like a queen on her island throne.

If we were to take out of the world to-day the means of livelihood which have been discovered during the last half-century, millions of our fellow-citizens would be driven to starvation. A half-century ago a large proportion of the poor of New York lived in cellars reeking with filth and foul with every abomination. The whole world has been lifted to a new and larger life.

There is care now for sailors, for worthy employees, and for other laborers such as was unknown half a century ago. The world is swinging forward into a brighter light and a more fraternal and Christlike life than any of which our fathers ever dreamed. We are recognizing God now as our Father and all men as our brothers as no church of any name recognized God and men even half a century ago.

Let this be a genuine jubilee; let us consecrate ourselves to God and to his work with profound gratitude for the past and with earnest hope and rare enthusiasm for the future. The century is closing not in darkness, but brightness; not in atheism, but in faith; not in pessimism, but in optimism; not in slavish obedience to Satan, but in joyous fellowship with Jesus Christ. The world was never so good as it is to-day, and it will be vastly better half a century later in its history. Let the jubilee trumpet blow; let the bells of hope and joy ring. Standing on the border-line marking the close of this half-century and separating between the nineteenth and twentieth centuries we shout:

> Ring in the valiant man and free,
> . . . . .
> Ring in the Christ that is to be.

Our hearts grow tender as we think of the noble men who occupied this pulpit and these pews, and who are now in the immediate presence of God; may their example inspire us to deeper devotion, to lowlier toil, and to warmer love! May we dedicate ourselves anew to God so that those who come after us may be inspired by our example to labor with Christly devotion for the honor of God and the salvation of men; and may we all at the last share in the celestial jubilee when all the bells of heaven shall ring with glad acclaim, and may we with saints and seraphs chant, "Blessing, and glory, and wisdom, and thanksgiving, and honor, and power, and might, be unto our God for ever and ever! Amen."

XVIII

THE DIVINE FORGIVENESS

"If we confess our sins, he is faithful and just to forgive us our sins, and to cleanse us from all unrighteousness." 1 John 1 : 9.

XVIII

THESE words have given comfort and inspiration to many doubting and fearful hearts. They have often come as a message from God himself to sinful and struggling souls. They sing themselves in our hearts now as strains of sweet and heavenly music. They might well have a place in the solemn litany of the most stately liturgy. They are often repeated by us in our private, our social, and our public prayers. They will never lose their meaning nor their inspiring ministry until this sinful world is fully converted to God. They stand in this scripture in close connection with the assertion that if we say we have no sin we are guilty of deceiving ourselves, and thus we prove that the truth is not in us. But while we are obliged to confess that we have sin, we may plead his gracious assurance of forgiveness, and we may cherish the joyous hope of being cleansed from all unrighteousness. No man in his senses will say in the sight of God that he is free from sin; but every penitent soul may go to God confessing his own guilt and pleading God's promise, and soon he will rejoice in the cleansing power of God's grace. Around three words suggested by the text the teaching of this scripture gathers —Confession, Forgiveness, Cleansing.

The first of these three words to be considered is *confession*. Divine forgiveness always presupposes human confession. We have no assurance that forgiveness will be imparted except full acknowledgment of sin be made. Confession as here emphasized is not simply confession of the mouth; neither is it simply contrition of the heart. There may be lip-confession without heart contrition, and heart-contrition without lip-confession. The desired outward confession springs from inward contrition; it is the heart voicing itself in confession with the mouth. The Apostle Paul teaches that, "with the heart man believeth unto righteousness, and with the mouth confession is made unto salvation."

To whom, then, is this genuine confession to be made? Manifestly to those whom we have injured. There is a sense in which we are to make confession to ourselves. Every unconverted man has wronged his own soul; every such man has sinned against the noblest instincts of his nature, against his intelligence, against his reason, and against his conscience. The Apostle Paul said to the alarmed jailer, "Do thyself no harm." This is the teaching of religion to every man concerning himself. It enjoins upon men to do themselves no harm by pernicious habits or by indulgence in sin of any kind. True religion seeks the highest welfare of all men. If this teaching were always and everywhere obeyed men would never do themselves harm. Every man who disobeys God dishonors himself. He takes the crown of noblest manhood from his own brow and tramples it in the dust. The true penitent is willing to go with a lighted candle through the chamber of his own soul. He is willing to humble himself before God that he may be exalted by God before men. Acts of this kind test a man's sincerity and reveal his true character. Many men do not wish to know themselves; they do not dare to be alone with themselves; they are afraid of the rebukes of their own conscience. They quail in the light which their own illumined judgment flashes upon their crooked paths and their sinful deeds. But the humbling revelation which such an examination produces is often the first step toward a full confession and toward eternal salvation.

Confession is also to be made to our fellowmen. Directly and indirectly in living a life of sin we have wronged others as well as ourselves. No man has a right to set a bad example; no man can live for himself. Every act is far-reaching in its immediate influence and in its ultimate consequences. One wrong act may start a circle of influences which will reach even to eternity, as a pebble dropped into the quiet lake starts ever-widening circles which reach the shore. This is a tremendous thought. It makes life real and terrible, if it is a life of sin; it makes life rich and glorious, if it is spent in the service of God. This fact suggests a terrible law. The guilt of one person involves many in its consequences. If a man could sin and suffer alone, sin would still be bad enough; but since the innocent must suffer with the guilty, sin becomes unspeakably sinful and terrible. The law which has its illustration in these experiences is universal and immutable as gravitation. If you refuse Christ to-day you not only injure yourself, but you injure all your friends and neighbors. Disobedience to God is injury to man. A full and frank confession to those we have wronged is manly and divine. The unmanliness consists in the perpetration of the wrong. The guilt of our sin, and not the confession of that sin, should suffuse our cheek with shame. We often act as if the shame of sin was in its discovery and not in its committal. Peace of mind cannot be secured until the wrong is confessed and the sin is forgiven. The laws of nature as well as the moral laws of God teach this great lesson.

But to God especially is our confession to be made. This form of confession includes all other elements of confession. There can be no true confession to ourselves or to our fellow-men except as there has been confession unto God. If we have not made confession to him, our confession to man is practically insincere and so worthless. When we turn to the two great penitential psalms, the thirty-second and the fifty-first, this lesson is made clear, and this element in confession is made most emphatic. David had sinned against many others as well as against God. He had offended against human laws and against the recognized principles of social life. His sin against Uriah and his family was deep, dark, and devilish; but still he says to God, "Against thee, thee only have I sinned and done evil in thy sight." The chief heinousness of his offense was in its violation of the law of God. Every true penitent can understand the significance of this strong language on the part of the royal penitent and psalmist. He did not make this confession simply because his sin might bring to him poverty, but chiefly because it was an offense against the pure and holy God; because it was a violation of his law and was offensive to the last degree in God's sight. Except there be this element in confession we may well doubt its sincerity. Every deeply penitent soul is ready to say unto God with the brokenhearted David, "Against thee, thee only have I sinned." The same great truth is taught us in the words of the prodigal son as he is returning to his father. He also recognized that his sin consisted chiefly in disobedience to that father and in departure from his home and heart. His words find a response still in the heart of every true penitent: "Father, I have sinned against heaven and before thee." God help us to recognize our sinfulness against him, and to introduce this element into our confession as the honest expression of the contrition of our hearts.

The second great word suggested by this text is *forgiveness*. As we examine the text we discover that there is a conditional element in the forgiveness here suggested, "If we confess." Always in the word of God pardon implies confession. This implication is not an arbitrary command on the part of God. God's commands are sovereign, but never arbitrary or capricious. There are profound reasons underlying all God's requirements. If we could see as God sees, we would always do as God does. If we could know as God knows, we would always demand what God demands. The laws of nature are not contradictory to the laws of grace. Revelation introduces us into a higher sphere than creation, but the lessons taught in both spheres are harmonious. To our limited vision and restricted faculties some of God's laws may seem to be arbitrary; but if our vision were broader and our faculties more acute we would see that God's sovereign demands are in harmony with the dictates of the highest reason. There can be no real forgiveness except there be true confession. Only the penitent's heart can receive divine peace as the result of forgiveness. So long as men are impenitent even the great and merciful God cannot bestow upon them true forgiveness. God would be practically casting pearls before swine if he offered men the treasures of forgiving grace before they showed their preparation for his mercy by the sincerity of their penitence. God's method of pardoning is thus seen to be in harmony with the highest reasoning and with the scientific conclusions of rational minds.

But when the human condition is met the divine forgiveness is assured. We are here taught that God is faithful in bestowing forgiveness. He is faithful to his plighted word and to his oft-repeated promises; he will assuredly grant us the forgiveness which he has so graciously promised. God cannot deny himself; than this truth nothing is more certain. When we make humble and hearty confession of our sins we cast ourselves in Christ's appointed way on God for forgiveness, and we must thus attest the faithfulness of his promises in granting us his forgiveness. If we can trust God for anything it is for the full and free forgiveness of sin when we have complied with his requirements. That he might cleanse us from all sin Christ came into the world, lived his life of obedience to

v

God, and died as the Atoner for sin. He sits at the right hand of the Majesty on high now to give repentance and remission of sin. We may put full faith in his willingness and ability to grant us remission.

But, furthermore, he is just in bestowing forgiveness as well as faithful. The forgiveness which he imparts is justifiable forgiveness. God must be just or cease to be God. We cannot for a moment think of God as unjust. One act of injustice on the part of God would overthrow his throne and leave this universe without a judge, without a father, without a Saviour, without a God. The attribute of absolute justice is inseparable from all true ideas of the God and Father of our Lord Jesus Christ. In bestowing his mercy he will be true to his promises. He will be just to his Son in the covenant of redemption, and he will be just to men who have put their implicit trust in Jesus Christ. The atonement of Jesus Christ satisfies our sense of justice and enables us to see how God can now be just while he is the justifier of those who believe in Jesus Christ.

The Apostle Paul clearly teaches the possibility of perfect harmony between God's attributes of justice and mercy. This great truth the apostle brings out in his letter to the Romans, the third chapter and the twenty-sixth verse. That verse is in many respects the very essence of the gospel. It shows that God retains the integrity of his character while he remits the penalty due to sinners; it shows that he can forgive sinners being penitent without sacrificing his divine and eternal justice. By giving his Son as a substitute for sinners he now can forgive sinners while he maintains the integrity of the divine law against sin. The salvation of men at the expense of the justice of God is unthinkable. No human intellect, however lofty or profound, could have answered the question, "How should man be just with God?" This question staggered all thinkers in all ages. It has been the great inquiry ever before the mind of earnest students. Every man knows that he is a sinner, and must feel that God would be just in inflicting punishment proportioned to his guilt. The effort to answer this question has given rise to all the forms of religion among men; to all the penances and sacrifices of different faiths among many nations. But only in the Christian revelation can the answer be found; only through the infinite merits of the Redeemer can men conscious of their guilt be forgiven while God's law is honored and their own sense of justice is satisfied.

The third word around which the thoughts of the text gather in appropriate order is *cleansing*. The characteristics of the cleansing here promised are worthy of our attentive consideration

To cleanse is more than merely to forgive. We see at once that we have advanced a step in our consideration of God's wonderful grace to the children of men. Forgiveness were much, forgiveness were an indescribable blessing; but cleansing introduces us into a nobler condition and a sweeter relation. To forgive is to justify; but to cleanse is to sanctify as well as justify. It is a mark of wonderful condescension on the part of God, and a token of marvelous blessing in our own experience. For cleansing as well as forgiveness we must earnestly seek; for purification as well as pardon we must constantly strive.

Careful study of the text shows us that it is a personal cleansing. The promise is that he will cleanse us from all unrighteousness. We must personally be washed in the precious blood of the Son of God. Religion is intensely personal. A wall high as heaven and deep as hell separates every personality from every other. Personality is eternal. Individuality outlives death and the judgment. Moses and Elijah were Moses and Elijah though they had been respectively about one thousand five hundred and one thousand years in heaven. We cannot be saved because of the righteousness of others. There must be a personal cleansing in the fountain opened for sin and cleansing. To that fountain I now invite you. Oh, come, wash and be clean now; yea, wash and be whiter than snow! It is God's desire that every man should be justified, that every man should be saved with an eternal salvation.

It is observable also, that this is divine cleansing; for it is God who is here represented as forgiving and cleansing. He alone can cleanse from sin. Only the blood of Jesus Christ his Son possesses cleansing power. The fountains of earth can never wash away the sins of men. As well might an Ethiopian attempt "by nitre and much soap" to make himself white, as for a sinner to expect to make himself white by any application of his own merits and righteousness. As a ground of salvation all our doings are deadly; no man can be saved by good works as a ground of acceptance with God. Good works are the fruit of the faith implanted in the soul. There is only one fountain that can wash away the stain of sin. Oh, come to that fountain here and now, wash and be clean! We observe also that it is a perfect cleansing—" cleanse us from all unrighteousness." The sin which abides in the heart as conscious guilt may be removed by God's pardon. The sin which abides in us as pollution requires divine cleansing. All men might receive forgiveness and cleansing if they would but confess their guilt and receive divine mercy. There is no sin so dark but that the blood of Christ can wash it away; there is no heart so foul but that it may be made whiter than the driven snow. Every form of unrighteousness is sin, and as such is to be cleansed from the soul. It is the duty and privilege of every child of God to have his heart cleansed from remaining depravity, and to keep himself unspotted from the world and in sweet fellowship with his Redeemer.

Do I here advocate doctrines of sinless perfection? If I did, the verse following the text would rebuke me and contradict my teaching. In that verse it is distinctly said, "If we say that we have not sinned we make God a liar, and his word is not in us." No man may claim sinless perfection. Such a claim as this the Apostle Paul never made, but distinctly repudiated; but although men ought not to claim that they have attained to a sinless life, it is certain that all of us might live a much higher life than we do now. It is a false humility which insists on calling ourselves servants, when God calls us sons and daughters. By being cleansed from all unrighteousness we are certainly taught that we may have all kinds, classes, and degrees of sin forgiven; that there is no stain so dark or deep that the blood of Christ cannot take it away. Think of the various classes of saved sinners mentioned in the Bible. Almost every possible condition of life is represented among the redeemed, whose salvation is described on the inspired page. Here are the men and women who were outcasts from society, whose hands were red with blood, whose honor was trampled in the dust, whose purity was as a flower stained and rejected, but the grace of God cleansed them from sin and enrolled them among the heroes and heroines of faith. Behold the blood-washed throng before the great white throne. They are there from every nation ; they are there cleansed from every kind and degree of sin. The fountain is still open ; its cleansing tide flowing full and free. I stand here to-day finding, as John the Baptist found, my highest joy, my sweetest privilege, and my most solemn duty in pointing to Jesus Christ and saying, " Behold, the Lamb of God, which taketh away the sin of the world."

Having looked to Jesus in penitence and faith let us not doubt the reality of our forgiveness. If one of our children had offended against us, had made hearty confession, and had received our full forgiveness, we certainly should not expect him to ask day by day, " Father, am I forgiven or not?" Such questioning would imply such unbelief on his part as would wound all our parental sensibilities. When God has granted his pardon we surely ought not longer to doubt his word. Can we not believe the word of the loving, the gracious, and the unchangeable God? Why should our hearts be left open to new doubts and fears ? Why should we trust our own mutable feelings rather than the word of the immutable Jehovah? Let us sweetly, joyously, triumphantly rest our wavering hearts on the promise of our God. He cannot deny himself. Our doubts disturb our joys and dishonor our Saviour. Let us know that "the word of our God shall stand for ever."

XIX

THE PERFECTED LIGHT

"But the path of the just is as the shining light, that shineth more and more unto the perfect day." Prov. 4 : 18.

XIX

WE do not know with absolute certainty whether these are the words of David to Solomon or of Solomon directly to us. It matters little, however, what conclusion we may reach on that point; in either case they are the words of God to us. This verse lies between two verses descriptive of the conduct and condition of the wicked. In the previous verse they are represented as eating the bread of wickedness and drinking the wine of violence; and in the verse following the text their way is described as darkness and they as stumbling at they know not what. It would be difficult to find anywhere a more expressive description of the wretched condition of wicked men. It is bad enough for men to stumble when they know the nature of their stumbling-block; but this description makes a powerful appeal to the imagination, and it conjures up all imaginable dangers and evils in which wicked men flounder about in the dark. Beautiful in contrast with what precedes and with what follows is the description of the just in the text. God's people are here called the "just." They are the subjects of divine grace, are created anew in

Christ Jesus, in righteousness and true holiness. They have been justified by faith from all things from which they could not be justified by the law of Moses. Life is spoken of here, as it so often is in Scripture, as a path. In both Testaments human life is represented as a way or path, and human conduct as walking in this way or path. In harmony with this idea we are exhorted to walk circumspectly, honestly, and soberly; and, according to the same usage, we are spoken of as walking in love and walking in the light. All these various phrases indicate the course of human life. We may understand then, by the expression "the path of the just," the earthly life, the daily experience, the whole course of a Christian's earthly existence.

What, then, are the characteristics of this path as indicated in the text? In a general way we know that it is bright and beautiful, while that of the wicked is dark and dangerous; but the text allows us to go more fully into particulars.

The text teaches us, in the first place, that this *path is as a shining light.* We have in this complete description a remarkably fine figure. We see the sun rising in the eastern sky, whose curtains of crimson and gold are lifted to welcome his approach. No sight is more glorious than that of the sun rising and going forth in his might. The psalmist caught this beautiful idea when he described, in the nineteenth Psalm, its brilliant advent, "as a bridegroom going out of his chamber, and rejoicing as a strong man to run a race." Breezes chant their matin songs to welcome the coming of the king of day, and dewdrops like diamonds glisten on the earth's green carpet, reflecting the sun's beauty and glory in their tiny orbs. Familiarity robs this scene of its transcendent beauty, and of much of its grandeur; but all of us are conscious of its influence as often as we behold the wonderful picture. We need not wonder that many heathen nations worshiped the god of day; we need not wonder that even now men turn with wonder and with an admiration akin to reverence to the light-giving sun as he moves forward in his career.

The figure in the text, however, is not limited to the rising of the sun; it contemplates this dazzling orb as still climbing the heavens in majestic splendor. It suggests the coming of the noon-day hour, and the continuous progress to that hour of the king of day as a mighty conqueror marching in regal glory. The figure ends with the perfected day, and does not include the sun's descent along the western sky. It leaves us in the full and blinding glory of the sun's noonday brilliancy. The thought is overwhelming that century after century the sun has trodden this path of splendor and glory, pouring out its burning heat, its blinding light, and its life-giving rays without weakness or weariness, without suspension or exhaustion.

To such glory as this the brightness of the Christian's path is here likened. Is this statement too strong? Do our experience and observation justify this glowing figure? These questions are worthy of careful answers.

The path of Christians is a shining light unto themselves. The day of conversion was to many a day of transformation; it was the time when the darkness of doubt and unbelief fled away, and when the glorious light of hope and joy shone with undimmed splendor on their path. Christ's uplifted countenance gave them unspeakable joy and unbroken peace. The Christian still sees his own vileness, but at the same time he sees and wears the spotless robe of Christ's righteousness. Christ is his way, his truth, his light, and his life; and in him is no darkness at all. All Christians realize that the word of God is a lamp unto their feet and a light unto their path. Believers are themselves light in the Lord; we are distinctly taught that they walk in the light even as he is in the light. They are not left long in darkness as to their duty; no willing and obedient heart is ever left long in doubt as to faith or practice. Whosoever is willing to obey Christ's law shall assuredly know Christ's doctrine. We may not have the light far ahead; but we shall have light for the next step, and when that is taken, there shall be light for the next, and the next, and so we shall move forward to the end of our course. The true Christian may always offer this prayer, so beautiful in itself and so suggestive in its origin and associations:

> Lead, kindly Light! amid th' encircling gloom,
>   Lead thou me on;
> The night is dark, and I am far from home,
>   Lead thou me on;
> Keep thou my feet: I do not ask to see
> The distant scene; one step enough for me.

The path of the Christian is, furthermore, a shining light for others. Christians are the light of the world; this great honor is given them by the Lord himself. There is a sense in which they are themselves luminous bodies shining "amid the encircling gloom." It has often been pointed out that Christians partake of some of the qualities of the two kinds of luminous bodies known to us. The first of these bodies are the sun and the fixed stars; these have light in themselves, light inherently, light independently of other bodies. The second kind of luminous bodies are the moon and the planets; they shine by reflected light. True Christians, as before suggested, resemble both these bodies.

In one sense they have no inherent light, but by nature are utterly dark. Their present light is like that of the second class of luminous bodies, derived and not inherent; but when they are illuminated they are more than mere reflectors, for they become themselves centers of light, heat, and life. They send out brilliant rays to guide others in the path of duty and joy. It is interesting and instructive to observe that Christ uses language concerning his people which he used as descriptive of himself. Of himself he said, "I am the light of the world"; and of his disciples he said, "Ye are the light of the world." We are in some measure, and it is here said with deep humility, Christ to the world. Every believer, in some sense, is Jesus Christ to souls about him who are in darkness and death. We thus represent God to this fallen and sinful world. All that many men know of God they learn of us. An inspired apostle has said, "God who commanded the light to shine out of darkness hath shined in our hearts, to give the light of the knowledge of the glory of God in the face of Jesus Christ." The blessed Master said, "Let your light so shine before men, that they may see your good works, and glorify your Father which is heaven." Some believers are but as tallow dips, others as molded candles, others as oil lamps, others as street gas-lamps, and still others are as electric lights of great height and of wonderful brilliancy. In the case of some, owing to intellectual attainments and social position, the light is intense, is bright. For many elements of our light-giving power we may not be largely responsible; but in all cases we are commanded to let our light shine, whether it be large or little and whether it be placed high or be relatively or actually low. We must cause our light to shine upon the pathway of others, that they may be led into the service of God here and into the immediate presence of God hereafter.

It thus comes to pass that the path of Christians is a shining light to reveal the glory of God to the world. They walk along an illuminated pathway; they leave a track of light and glory behind them. They are the noblest beings on this side of heaven; they are God's illuminated, and so God's shining ones; they embody and declare more of God's glory than all the works of God's hands. God is known by his works, for no man hath seen him at any time. The visible things of God, as the Apostle Paul teaches, declare the invisible things of God. All God's revelations are intended to lead up to spiritual apprehensions of himself. This is true in revelation as in creation. In revelation the prophets pointed to John the Baptist, and John the Baptist pointed to Jesus the Christ, and Jesus himself finally pointed to the Holy Spirit as the divine illuminator of darkened souls. All forms of inanimate creation proclaim God. All over this universe he has written himself in the glory of his power, in the greatness of his wisdom, and in the infiniteness of his love. This truth, the Apostle Paul reminds us, even thoughtful heathen could understand and appreciate. The undevout student of nature is an inaccurate student of nature. The genuine rationalist is he who studies natural law and phenomena in the light of revealed truth and of Christian interpretation. The man who puts himself outside of the light of God in the face of Jesus Christ is undeserving the title of rationalist. He is irrational in his thinking and must inevitably be illogical in his conclusions.

There is an ascending scale of beings in whom God displays his glory. Living beings reveal it more fully than inanimate objects. The cattle, the fowl, and the creeping things all in their measure make known God in his creative power and in his providential wisdom. But when we come to responsible, intelligent, and immortal men we rise to a much higher stage. Man is the crowning glory of God's creative wisdom; he stands king on the pedestal of creative power and of infinite wisdom. To him all beings below him may well look up with wonder and admiration. He stands above them as made in the image of his God, and as a possible heir of God and a joint-heir with Jesus Christ. One of the Greek names for man strictly means the upward-looking being. The more man is developed on all sides of his nature the more of God's glory it is possible for him to display. In man as redeemed by Jesus Christ, as cleansed in his precious blood, and as made a candidate for heaven, we have God's grandest and divinest manifestation of himself.

We are clearly taught that the church makes to the universe the greatest display of God's manifold wisdom. The church is the bride of Jesus Christ; she goes through this world with the robe of his righteousness falling in graceful folds from her shoulders, with the crown of his glory on her brow, and leaning lovingly on his arm while she walks triumphantly by his side. Christian men and women are living epistles, known and read of all men, making known God's saving power; they are trophies of his sovereign grace and eternal love; and they are proofs of God's power to overcome Satan and to triumph over all forms of darkness. It is not too much to say that they are the very climax of God's wonderful works, astonishing angels and silencing devils. God's children are probably more like God than are any other created beings. While Jesus Christ is God's Son by a mysterious generation, they are God's sons by adoption, by regeneration, and so they are partakers of the divine nature. Let us not hesitate to say that they are actually begotten of God and that thus his divine life is in their souls. They stand next to Jesus Christ, who is the brightness of his glory and the express image of his person. Here and now they are the sons of God; not simply his sons by adoption—that were much, that were a marvelous attainment; but they are actually his sons by the impartation of his divine nature. Can we rise to the greatness of this Alpine peak of possibility and attainment? May we not with holy boldness dare claim our privileges as the sons and daughters of the Lord Almighty? Oh, how glorious it is to be a child of God, an heir of heaven, and a joint-heir with Jesus Christ! Let us remember, O men and women, that the world judges our Father by his children, and let us see to it, as we meet to-day in his house, as we are gathered about this table on which are spread the memorials of Christ's death, that we do not misrepresent our heavenly Father nor dishonor our Elder Brother.

The second characteristic of this path is that *it is an increasing light*—"that shineth more and more." The Christian's life is progressive. He must never be satisfied with his present attainments; he must ever remember that there are before him loftier heights yet to be reached. The Christian's life, in another passage of Scripture, is compared to the sun when "he goeth forth." Christians also must continually advance. The Apostle Paul was far from feeling that he had attained or was already perfect. The more of true grace believers possess, the more of true grace they desire to possess. They do not look back to their conversion as the strongest evidence of their conversion. Every true believer has made vast progress since the time when he first began the Christian life. Each day Christians ought to give new proof to themselves and to others that they are the children of God. The Christian is in a lamentable condition who is looking away back through the years to the time of his conversion for the proofs of his adoption into the family of God. Such a man is to be profoundly pitied, and at the same time he is to be earnestly but kindly rebuked. Glorious as were those first experiences, they have been vastly surpassed by those of a later day. The old soldier is better than the raw recruit. The true believer knows how to watch and pray, to fight and to triumph, as the young convert neither did nor could expect to know. It is readily granted that there is a rare tenderness, freshness, and sweetness in one's first love; but it must also be emphatically affirmed that there is a ripeness, maturity, and fullness in one's late love which the early love could not possess.

All the figures of Scripture used to illustrate the progress of the Christian life, directly or indirectly, emphasize the law of growth.

The godly man is represented as a tree "that bringeth forth his fruit in his season." Elsewhere it is said of him, "He shall flourish like the palm tree; he shall grow like a cedar in Lebanon"; and still elsewhere he is represented as growing as the vine and the lily. The simile of a race that is often used in this connection implies continuous progress. So do all these architectural images which speak of foundations and building thereon. Growth is important because it affects our conditions hereafter as well as here. Nothing is more certain than that there are degrees in glory as in suffering; nothing is more certain than that "one star differeth from another star in glory." Among the saved there are those who were brought in at the eleventh hour, those that are barely saved; but to others there is given an abundant entrance among the shining hosts of heaven.

Except there be growth in the Christian life, the most conclusive evidence of the existence of Christian life is wanting. Let this test be carefully applied to all our experiences at this moment. Let us revert once more to the figure which underlies the text of this morning; our path is to be as the light that shineth more and more. This figure suggests the gradual increase of the light occasioned by the sun's rays according to the laws of atmospheric reflection. Do you know that you love God, his word, his house, his altar, his services better than you did a month ago? Let me press this question home upon heart and conscience this morning. If you are not advancing you are retrograding. It is absolutely impossible to remain long stationary. In traveling in the Christian path a believer is like a man on a bicycle—he must go on or very soon go off. Let the heart just now be honest with itself in making a comparison in this practical way between the attainments of to-day and those of a month ago. Growth in the Christian life must follow the laws of growth everywhere. A plant in a dark cellar must either die or live a poor, feeble, and dying life. It needs light; it needs sunshine. If you live in the dark cellar of your own nature you will grow more and more feeble, until spiritual death succeeds to the long absence of spiritual life and power. If you live in the shadows of doubt, in the gloomy vales of misanthropy, in the dark dens of fault-finding and selfishness, you will lose all the light and joy, and finally the very life of the true believer. Come out into God's sweet sunshine this morning. Eat the divine manna as given in the divine book. Exercise all the spiritual sympathies and muscles by following Christ, "who went about doing good."

Arouse yourself to go for some poor fellow-Christian, some poor, struggling, dying fellow-being in life's terrible journey, and you will soon find the warm life-blood of a true humanity, and of a divine impartation once more coursing through your veins. Your Jeremiads will be changed into hallelujahs, and you yourself will leave the vale of gloom and shout on the mountain tops of light and joy.

In the last place, we see that *this light will one day be perfected*—"unto the perfect day." The figure underlying the text suggests the perfection of the noonday light. The sun climbs the eastern sky until he is clearly elevated above the horizon, and then the prepared, or perfected, day has come. One interpreter has rendered the passage by the words, "going and illuminating until the prepared day." The believer's final victory and glory are the result of a long and careful preparation on the part of God, and secondarily, on his own part. The perfection of that day is due in part to this element of preparedness, of which mention is here made. The man of God is only in his twilight here; he is preparing for the realms of everlasting light and day. Now he is walking in earth's shadows; but the time will come when he will enter into the full light and glory of heavenly brightness and felicity.

There will then be perfect light on all the

mysterious providences of God which come to us in our earthly pilgrimage. The purpose of God, as unfolded in these providences, we cannot now fully understand; they are to us as if printed in characters that are upside down, but when we reach the other world and look back upon these mysterious providences, our viewpoint will have so completely changed that we can read them with perfect ease, and with meaning which will fill our souls with joy unspeakable as we sing our song of praise to him that doeth all things well. There will then be fuller light on all the wonders of God's character, on all the mysteries and glories of God's redemptive grace; on all the progressive steps of God's revelation from paradise lost to paradise restored. We shall then see that all this world's history is but a hyphen between the garden of Eden and the paradise of God. We shall have perfect light on all the steps of our own progress in the divine light and likeness. We know something even now, not only of our present dignity, but of our future glory. We know even now that when we shall see Jesus, we shall be like him. Marvelous thought! Transcendent possibility! What angel may fathom the depths of so profound a truth as this? What angel may scale the heights of so lofty a possibility as this? Perhaps we shall be like Christ in breadth, depth, height, and splendor of intellect; perhaps we shall be like him in purity, nobility, and divinity of character. Perhaps we shall be like him in unbroken peace, unclouded happiness, unblemished purity, and unfading glory.

Once more we are reminded of the striking contrast here suggested between the righteous and the wicked. Oh, the unspeakable folly of those who eat the bread of wickedness and drink the wine of violence! Oh, the unspeakable wretchedness of the wicked whose way is as darkness, and who know not at what they stumble as they go groping in the dark! While it is true, as we see, that the light in which Christians walk here is but the prophecy of that brighter light which they shall enjoy when they shall shine as the sun, it is also true that the darkness of the wicked here is but the prophecy of that deeper darkness in which at the last they shall dwell. There are no more solemn words than these, "cast into outer darkness." The vagueness of this region appeals to the imagination. The absence of definite description adds to the awfulness of the condition. This darkness was never intended for men, but for the devil and his angels. Oh, why will men determine to have their abode with demons? Turn ye, turn ye today into this path of light and love, of peace and joy, of pleasure and purity. Then at the last, amid the splendors of heaven, you shall shine above the brightness of the sun.

XX

THE REALIZED IDEAL

"Beloved, now are we the sons of God, and it doth not yet appear what we shall be: but we know that, when he shall appear, we shall be like him; for we shall see him as he is."   *1 John 3 : 2.*

XX

WE have often described the Apostle Peter as the apostle of hope, the Apostle Paul as the apostle of logic, and the Apostle John as the apostle of love. We must not, however, suppose that in so describing these apostles we exclude other commendable qualities which we know they possessed. There was a vast amount of logic and love in Peter's hope; there was a great degree of hope and love in Paul's logic; and there was an equal amount of logic and hope in John's love.

Never did John forget his experience when he pillowed his head on the bosom of Jesus. He listened to the music of Christ's voice, tuned to tenderest love, and uttered in softest accents of divinest affection. And so toward the close of his life John constantly strikes the note of love and sings this song in almost every chapter that he wrote. Tradition tells us that when at Ephesus, and so old and feeble that he could not go to the assemblies of the church without being carried by his disciples, and being unable to deliver long discourses, he was accustomed to say, "Little children, love one another"; and when some wondered why he so often repeated that exhortation, his answer was, "This is what the Lord commands you; and this, if you do it, is sufficient." There is in this exhortation an echo of the words of Jesus, and a corroboration of the teachings of Paul. As I read these closing Epistles of John I find that there is but little of John left; almost all in his life is Jesus. John was passing into the shadow; Jesus was coming out into fuller and brighter light. John was joyously decreasing; Christ was gloriously increasing. Thus all through these chapters we hear the echo of Christ's words spoken years before.

We are not surprised, therefore, that he opens this chapter by saying, "Behold, what manner of love the Father hath bestowed on us." It is an interesting fact that nowhere in the Bible is there any attempt made to give us a statement of the measure of God's love. If any man might know that love, that man would truly be the Apostle John. He did know much of it; he had grasped the hand, looked into the eyes, listened to the voice, and felt the throbbing of the heart of Jesus Christ. But even he does not attempt to give us the measure of love; all that he can say is, "Behold, what manner of love the Father hath bestowed upon us, that we should be called the sons of God." If any other man might know the measurement of God's love that man would be the peerless Paul. But he nowhere attempts to give its measure. He is awed, charmed, overwhelmed by the love of God in Christ Jesus. It constrained him to live and die for Christ. He was assured that no created thing could separate him from that wondrous, mighty, and eternal love. He spoke eloquently of its breadth, length, depth, and height. He prayed that we might know it; but he immediately declares that it " passeth knowledge." He cannot tell fully its greatness, any more than could the Apostle John, who can only speak of its manner, and not of its measure. And now, passing from the precious thought of God's unmeasured and unmeasurable love, the beloved apostle comes to the blessings which that love has secured for the children of God; and these blessings he beautifully enumerates in my text: " Beloved, now are we sons of God, and it doth not yet appear what we shall be; but we know that when he shall appear, we shall be like him; for we shall see him as he is."

Allow me, in developing these glorious truths, to call attention, in the first place, to *the present privileges of true believers.* " Beloved, now are we the sons of God." In looking at this category of blessings we discover that the first element in it is that we are called " beloved " by an inspired apostle, and such an apostle as was John. A little time ago that thought came to me with special force. It surely is a great thing to be honored by honorable men; to be beloved by beloved men; but still it is a greater thing to be beloved by an inspired and almost divine man, as was the noble John. The people of God are known in the word of God by many titles. They are called children, because they are born from above by the Spirit of God; they also are led by the Spirit of God, and conscious of their new filial relationship they cry, Abba, Father. They are called believers, because faith in Christ is a controlling element in their new and gracious life. They are called disciples, because as pupils they sit at Jesus' feet and learn of him to be meek and lowly in heart, and thus they find rest to their souls. They are called brethren, because a fraternal spirit governs all their relations with one another. They are called heirs of God because as members of his family and joint-heirs with Christ they are to receive a triple crown. Their manifold relations with God and with one another are indicated by many names. Even in the Old Testament we read, "for so he giveth his beloved sleep"; and "beloved" is the title which the apostle here gives to God's children. It is a great blessing to be worthy of the confidence, esteem, and affection of good men. That man is to be envied whose character entitles him to the affection of high-minded men and of pure-hearted women. That man is to be pitied and blamed, who, having enjoyed this high honor, forfeits it by unworthiness of character. I beseech you, who are the children of God, that you never so speak, never so act, never so think, as to be, or even to seem to be, unworthy of your high title of sons and daughters of God, heirs of God, and joint-heirs with Jesus Christ! Oh, be worthy of that lofty designation, that glorious appellation; be worthy of that glorious crown of gold which awaits you; wear right royally that triple crown which God has prepared for the victors in the good fight, the crown of life, the crown of righteousness, and the crown of glory.

Another privilege of true believers, in this connection, is that they are called "the sons of God." We have perhaps seldom risen to the height of meaning contained in this expression. In the eighth of Romans reference is made to our adoption. Adoption is a great and precious truth; but it is not the whole truth concerning the relation of the children of God to their Father in heaven. Adoption indicates a new relationship with God; but regeneration teaches that a new creation by the Spirit of God has been experienced. Adoption implies regeneration, but regeneration necessarily includes adoption. You may adopt a child from the street and give that child your name; but adoption would not give that child your flesh and blood, your very nature; it would not make the child truly part of yourself. We know, however, that when God adopts he regenerates. It certainly is true that God is not satisfied with merely bringing us into his family by an act of adoption; he make us like his family; he imparts to us his own nature. We are begotten of God; we are made literally partakers of the divine nature. That is a wonderful truth; so wonderful that we could scarcely believe it, were we not distinctly so taught by the inspiration of God in Holy Scripture. We seldom rise to the full height of this gracious truth. We are actually made a part of God; we are actually begotten by God; he becomes more really our Father than is our earthly father. God's nature is imparted to us, and we actually become by regeneration the sons and daughters of God. This is a wonderful statement. I wish I could take its full meaning into my own heart; I wish I could impart all of its significance to other minds and hearts. Oh, realize to-day how great, how transcendent is the glory which God has already conferred upon you.

A Christian is the highest style of man; a Christian is a man who is Christlike in character; a man who is Christlike in aim and in love, and who one day will be wholly like him when he shall see Christ as he is. Every Christian has now much in possession, but he has still greater things in prospect; thought cannot conceive, much less can language express, all that God has in reserve for his redeemed children. Indeed, only those who are born again can truly address God as "Father," in the full meaning of the title; only they "who are led by the Spirit of God, are the sons of God"; only they who have received the spirit of adoption can truly cry "Abba, Father." Only in a vague sense can unregenerate men say, "Our Father, who art in heaven." They can call God a father only as a wandering, self-willed, disobedient child, who has, like another prodigal, gone into a far country, can apply the endearing name to the father in the old home, when he has forgotten that father's counsels, despised his reproofs, and well-nigh broken his heart. O wanderer, come home now. Come now into the possession of the great, the divine privilege of being a son or a daughter of God.

We ought also to emphasize the precious thought that this inestimable privilege is ours here and now—"Beloved, now are we the sons of God." We have erred in not taking into our hearts the blessed truth that this privilege is ours now. We have sometimes thought that to claim this promise now would be presumptuous. We have thought that to speak doubtfully was a mark of humility. Not so; it is rather a mark of unbelief. True humility takes the place which God assigns; it receives the blessings which God bestows. It is unbelief and not humility which uses "peradventures," "perhapses," and "ifs." Does not a man know that he loves God as certainly as that he loves his mother, his wife, or his child? Can he not test his love in practical ways in the one case as truly as in the other? Away with this false humility! Let us receive the honors our Father gives. Let us be children, and not merely servants. This morning, believer, though you be full of doubts and fears, you are a child of God; just now, though sorrows have come to your home and to your heart, you are a child of God; just now, though business perplexities multiply, you are a child of God; just now, though conscious of weakness and sin; just now, though at times obliged to confess waywardness and doubt, you are a child of God. Let that sweet hope fill your heart now while I speak and remain with you as a divine benediction.

I beg you also to notice, in the second place, *the present limitations of true believers*—"It doth not yet appear what we shall be." Of course, it does not yet appear, and, of course, it could not yet appear. We are not capable of taking in all that God has in store for us. Human faculties cannot discern these spiritual realities here or hereafter. "Eye hath not seen, nor ear heard, neither have entered into the heart of man the things which God hath prepared for them that love him." You are yet but a babe in the kingdom of God. You will one day, in that glorious world, know as you are known and see as you are seen. Here we do not know God as he is, but as we are. We do not know even this world; how then can we know the world that is to come? We are surrounded by mystery here and now regarding the things of time and sense. The infinitely great is no more mysterious than the infinitely small. The telescope does not reveal worlds more marvelous than those which are revealed by the miscroscope. We are between oceans of mystery as we live on our narrow neck of land. During the past generation science has made marvelous discoveries; but every great discovery has simply revealed another sphere of mystery lying ever beyond. We push the limit of the known farther out into the unknown sea; and the sea rolls still beyond into limitless regions of the unknown.

"It doth not yet appear what we shall be." We do not know what it is for a spirit to live in a disembodied state; we have had no experience of such an existence. It doth not yet appear fully what we shall be in the glorified state. It doth not yet appear what we shall be in the immediate presence of God; it cannot yet appear. We could not take it in; we could not endure the sight. I have listened to strains of music in the "Messiah" so sweet that I felt that I could not endure anything more unless I had new faculties to enable me to bear the increased bliss. How then in my present state could I endure heaven? The harmony would exhaust every faculty. No mortal could bear such heavenly delights. Perhaps the sights of heaven would blind us; the glory would be too much for mortal sight, and the music would thrill us beyond endurance. I read a little time ago of a French vessel that was four years absent from France and was just returning. As the ship came homeward and was near the shore of France, the sailors were almost unfit for service because of their uncontrollable joy; as they came still nearer they took out various presents which they had brought for mothers, for wives, and for children, and displayed them on deck. They came nearer still, and suddenly they saw the shores of France, and up went the shout, "La belle France," "La belle France!" beautiful France, beautiful France! Soon they saw their wives, mothers, and children on the shore, and they were so helpless in their excited joy that the captain had to get others to help in the docking of the ship. I think if the curtain could lift to-day, and we could see the glory of the other land and our beloved ones on that shore, our friends, our children, our parents, we would be unfitted for duty. Thank God, it doth not appear what we shall be or what we shall see!

Notice, in the third place, *the present knowledge which true believers possess*—" We know that when he shall appear we shall be like him, for we shall see him as he is." Thank God, we know that Christ is to return; he is to be with us and we with him. He came once before in humiliation; he will come this time in glory. He came once as the despised and rejected of men; he will come this time receiving the plaudits of saints, the praises of angels, and the songs of seraphs. He will come as God has promised. Whatever truth God has sent down in a promise we may send up in a prayer; so let the church send up her petition to-day, " Even so, come, Lord Jesus." We know too, that we shall see him when he comes. That is a thought of joy and peculiar preciousness. We have often wished that we might see him; that thought thrills our souls to-day. There are times of exaltation when we have been on some mount of transfiguration, when we have almost seen him, times when we could almost touch the hem of his garment. At such times we, like Peter, wanted to linger long in the Master's presence. And we are taught, also, that we shall be like him. His body underwent great changes between his resurrection and his ascension. He was able to enter rooms through closed doors, and that power he did not seem to possess, at least did not often use, previous to his crucifixion and resurrection. Perhaps we shall have bodies like his. Painful and sick bodies shall be banished; crooked and deformed bodies will be all gone forever. Beautiful bodies shall be ours, bodies without spot, without wrinkle, without defect; glorified bodies shall be ours. This wonderful body shall be made over again like unto the glorious body of Jesus Christ. We shall perhaps also have marvelous intellectual endowments. As Luther long ago suggested, we look at God's providences now as they are presented to us with the type backward; and so we cannot read the meaning of his dealings with us. But yonder all mysteries shall be solved; yonder the writing will be plain. We shall look at it from another point of view. Oh, what blessed attainments we shall make! I tell you sometimes I become weary with the struggles of life, with its doubts, its perplexities, and with its unsolved and insoluble problems. And sometimes I wish I could plume my wings for the heavenward flight.

Then we shall know—even as we are known. We shall make attainments in holiness; of that fact there is no doubt. Perhaps we shall be like Christ in holiness of character. The very thought is bliss. Thus we press forward toward the mark of the prize of the high calling of God in Christ Jesus. Oh, that just now we might most sweetly take into our hearts the great and precious privileges of the children of God!

Then we shall follow the exhortation of the apostle given in this connection, to purify ourselves, even as he is pure. O child of God, will you live like a child of the earth? Child of glory, will you look at the attainments of this world, instead of looking to the glory yonder? Just now I exhort you to look unto Jesus, the author and finisher of our faith. Get a glimpse here and now of the King in his beauty. Behold even now the land that is afar off, and your heart shall long for the fuller sight, the brighter glory, and the nearer vision. Gaze now on Christ as your atoning Lord and Saviour, and then you shall forever see him as the chiefest among ten thousand and the One altogether lovely.

www.ingramcontent.com/pod-product-compliance
Lightning Source LLC
Chambersburg PA
CBHW031427230426
43668CB00007B/470